I am no longer accepting
things I cannot change. I am
changing the things I cannot
accept.

— Angela Davis

Do It *Well*!

Stand up straight and realize
who you are, that you tower
over your circumstances.

— Maya Angelou

Do It *Well*!

Timeless Wisdom to Enrich Every Day

Swami Kriyananda

Crystal Clarity Publishers
Nevada City, California

Crystal Clarity Publishers, Nevada City, California
Copyright © 2009 Hansa Trust
All rights reserved. Published 2009

Printed in China
ISBN: 978-1-56589-241-5

Cover photograph by Barbara Bingham
Cover design by Madhavi Eby and production by Renée Glenn Designs
Interior design and layout by Crystal Clarity Publishers

Library of Congress Cataloging-in-Publication Data
Kriyananda, Swami.
  Do It Well! : Timeless Wisdom to Enrich Every Day / Swami
Kriyananda (J. Donald Walters). — 1st ed.
    p. cm.
  ISBN 978-1-56589-241-5 (tradepaper)
  1. Self-actualization (Psychology) 2. Conduct of life. I. Title.

  BF637.S4.K75 2009
  294.5'432—dc22
                          2009031059

www.crystalclarity.com
clarity@crystalclarity.com
800-424-1055

Preface

How many times have you felt bewildered when facing a difficult period in your life? A good friend of mine who is at a personal crossroads recently said to me, "I wish God would just appear and tell me what to do!"

How rarely that happens as we might expect, but God does speak to us more often than we realize through the words of wise and impartial friends. Swami Kriyananda, through the sayings in *Do It Well!*, is just such a friend.

Having had the privilege of knowing him for over forty years, I've observed that Swamiji himself has faithfully practiced the precepts he recommends to others in this book. In the vernacular, he "walks his talk."

Through his practice, Kriyananda has mastered the art of living. In these wise and loving sayings, he has given us the tools to find the guidance we're seeking, so that we, too, can *Do It Well!*

Devi Novak

Introduction

The sayings in this book consist of lessons I myself have learned in life, whether by experience or through trial and error; sometimes by deep pain or disappointment; many times through an inner joy almost unbearable. Someone said to me many years ago, "*You* can write happy songs; you've never suffered." I replied, "On the contrary, it's because I *have* suffered that I've earned the right to express happiness." What I've presented here is the fruit of many years of thoughtfully directed living.

This represents a complete revision of a former book of mine, *Do It NOW!* Of the nearly one hundred books I have written so far in my life, *Do It NOW!* was always (until now, that is) one of my favorites—so much so, in fact, that when I first published it in 1995, I actually, in my eagerness to share it with others, paid the printing costs myself for five thousand copies and gave them away freely.

Today, fourteen years later, I offer this revised version both because of my continued enthusiasm for the book, and out of my continued growth in the insights

Introduction

it expresses. I ask you *as a favor to yourself*: Buy, beg, or borrow this collection of *pensées*. (But don't steal it!—see the saying for April 9!) Keep it on your nightstand or in your meditation room. Read from it every morning, and ponder, throughout the day, the thoughts expressed. If even one saying should spare you some of the pains I have experienced in my own life, I shall feel amply rewarded. For whatever tests you face or have faced, they will very likely resemble some that I, too, have known.

January

1

Resolve difficulties by raising your level of consciousness and focusing your mind at the point between the eyebrows: the seat of superconsciousness.

2

Smile with the eyes, not only with the lips.

3

When communicating face to face with others, express your thoughts also through your eyes. To rely only on words is to reduce communication by half.

4

Your *reactions* to events are more important for you than the events themselves. Make sure that you react always in such ways as to increase your inner peace and happiness.

January

5

When **conversing** with people, try always to talk *with* them, not merely *at* them.

6

When **laughing,** laugh from your heart. There is no joy in intellectual laughter. Indeed, such laughter is often only a snicker of disdain.

7

In **any controversy,** test the rightness of your stand by the way it affects your deeper feelings. Such feelings, and not the fickle emotions, can be trusted. If a feeling is calm and joyful, the stand you take will be right. If your feelings are agitated or negative, however, they will emphasize lower emotions, which are almost always wrong. Even happy emotions can distort judgment. Calm feeling alone is usually right.

January

8

Assuming that you want others to listen to you, show them first the respect of listening to what *they* have to say. Even if they say nothing, listen first.

9

Listen to the melodies birds sing: They express a happiness latent everywhere in Nature. Then reflect: You, too, are a part of that happiness, which is a first expression of omnipresent joy.

10

Watch your reactions to others. If you see in anyone some quality that you like, try to develop it in yourself. But if a quality displeases you, then instead of criticizing it, work to expunge it from your own nature. Remember, this world only mirrors back to us what we are in ourselves.

January

11

Listen to the subtle tones in your voice. Ask yourself why people's voices express so much variety. The mechanism of speech never changes. One might expect the tones of human voices to be as alike as trumpets! Yet each person has intonations that are uniquely his own. An American at the airport in Patna, India, once recognized me solely by my voice. He hadn't seen me in fifteen years, when I was a teenager; he didn't even know I was in India. Listen to your own voice. Try to eliminate from it any qualities you don't like. Sweeten it with kindness; brighten it by showing interest in everything; soften it by respect for others; warm it with considerateness for their needs.

12

To put warmth into your voice, relax it physically, then project out to others your concern for their well-being. Let your voice rise from the heart, flow smoothly through your vocal cords (never tensely, as if being thrust through fierce opposition!); then out to the world through your spiritual eye at the point between the eyebrows.

January

13

Look for qualities in others to appreciate. What you see in them is a reflection of what you are in yourself. The more you appreciate others, the more they will return your appreciation—like strings on a musical instrument, which vibrate sympathetically with kindred tones. But if what you see are qualities you dislike, it will be because you have the same unattractive qualities in yourself. Use your negative opinions of others, in this case, as goads to self-transformation.

14

If you find yourself becoming agitated, relax your heart; therein lies the origin of both calmness and excitement. The quality of feeling is the very essence of consciousness. Without feeling, one would be a mere mechanism, as materialistic scientists insist all of us are. Their dogma teaches that clear understanding demands that we eliminate all feeling. The dogma contains two basic errors: Without feeling, and also without self-awareness, there could be no life, for the whole universe is a projection of the Supreme Self, whose nature is Bliss. Two things there are that science will never be able to create: feeling of any kind, and self-awareness.

January

15

Live with greater awareness. Let your energy flow out to others from the center of your heart, and thence to all the world. Let your impact on others be always beneficial.

16

Keep your heart open to others, to circumstances, to life itself. Accept what comes of itself, for only by acceptance, first, of the fact that things are as they are can you hope to change things to what you'd like them to be.

17

Talk meaningfully. Never chatter, as if merely to let people know that you are present and would like to be accounted for! Watch your words; give them the luster of intelligence even when you are speaking in fun.

18

Cultivate the art of brevity. A single well-phrased sentence will be long remembered, whereas long discourses are often soon forgotten. In writing this book, too, I have tried to make every sentence as short and pithy as I could. Meandering sentences, like country paths, often lose themselves in the unkempt grass of tangled thinking.

19

To make your thoughts interesting, infuse melody into your voice. Flat speech indicates a flat personality. If you yourself are interested in what you say, concentrate on that interest, rather than only on the words you speak. Automatically, in that case, your voice will gain in cadence, color, and rhythm.

20

Laugh *with* others, never *at* them. Let them feel that you are their friend. Avoid the boisterous laughter so commonly heard at revels. By saying, Laugh with others, I refer to that softer, more intimate sound which comes with inner appreciation of others' company.

21

Choose your words with kindness, inviting receptivity and understanding. Think of what to say that will *help* others, and not merely stimulate them.

22

For clarity, edit at least mentally what you say or write — always placing emphasis on simplicity, directness, and even rhythm. Convoluted sentences merely bewilder the mind. I said this earlier, but clarity demands special attention. Try to think *with* your readers or listeners, taking into account their varied levels of understanding.

23

Think space when you speak. Give others the time to absorb your ideas.

24

Listen for the unexpressed thoughts and feelings behind people's words. Often what they say only masks their true intentions. A common tendency when speaking is to "test the water," first, to see if its temperature is right for swimming.

25

If you seek to communicate with others, seek also to *commune* with them. *Feel* their consciousness. Appreciate them for what they are and do, not only for what they say.

26

Don't let yourself be trapped in a time frame. The secret of flowing gracefully with life, with people, with events, and certainly with the process of aging, is to greet every new experience with a fresh, creative outlook.

27

Get rid of likes and dislikes. They only agitate the mind and prevent one from seeing things as they really are. Instead, practice constant inner contentment.

28

Say only what you mean. In your most casual speech, be sincere, and you'll find others listening to you, instead of letting their gaze wander off in furtive search of a clock.

29

If you truly want to communicate with others, don't speak only from your intellect: speak from your heart. Many of humanity's problems, in fact, would be solved if people learned the right balance between heart and head. This need for balance between the two is the psychological reason for the attraction between the sexes.

30

Live at this moment: Enjoy it; learn from it. Thus, through the passage of years, you'll not only develop golden memories, but will find it easier to develop *smriti* (divine memory), the classic Sanskrit definition of enlightenment.

31

Concentrate on your present commitments; don't dwell regretfully on past failures. Your life will keep on improving, if you do your best *this very moment.*

February

February

1

If someone challenges something right and good that you are doing, meet that challenge vigorously. Try not to be hurtful, however, and always be calm in your own defense. If the challenge is to yourself, rather than to a cause in which you believe, remain dispassionate, and accept the outcome without demur, whatever it may be. Remember, nothing can touch who you are, in your inner Self.

2

If someone impugns your honor, ignore him. If you cannot ignore, seek a graceful—even a humorous—way out, like the American who once met a challenge to a duel in France by selecting for weapons "apple pie at ten paces." After all, what is your "honor"? It is only an affirmation of ego: the very thing you need to conquer, if you would eliminate further suffering from your life. Suffice it that you act honorably. People's unflattering opinions of you are not your problem, but their own.

3

Think of time as a radiation outward from your own center. Past and future move not only like a river, but also in a circle around their center in the never-changing NOW.

4

Certain mental attitudes resemble bodily postures. Do you lean habitually forward, as if to grasp events before they happen? Do you lean backward, as if to distance yourself from others and from any unpleasantness? Do you habitually lean sideways, as if seeking a strategy for getting around some obstacle? Keep your bodily and mental attitudes upright, relaxed, and serene, and you'll find it easy to cope with every difficulty.

5

Give people the time they need to express themselves clearly. The rhythms of thought vary, but sincere self-expression often requires deliberation.

6

Your body is a temple—more truly so than any edifice built by hands. Enter therein daily; move in solemn procession up the aisle of the spine to God's high altar in the forehead, the seat of superconscious ecstasy.

7

Never lend money unless you can feel, in your heart, that you are giving the money away. This practice will spare you much grief. For as Shakespeare said (through Polonius in *Hamlet*), "Loan oft loseth both itself and friend." Tell God that you place the money in His hands. He will then see to it that you will not consequently lack. Be sensible, however, when lending. Make sure you are helping someone whose need is real. I've often pondered the case of movie actors who carelessly gave away large amounts of the money they were earning, but years later died in penury.

8

To be fully aware, look for the hidden realities behind appearances.

February

9

If someone insults or makes fun of you, thank him—even warmly—and say, "I appreciate your reminder that I'm very far from perfect. Since perfection is what I'd like to attain, I consider it no insult to be told I still have work to do."

10

Keep a constant conversation with God flowing in your heart. Address the Lord in the second person, as "You," not as "He" or "She," or even as the nowadays-stilted "Thou." Speak to God from your heart. Share every thought, every feeling with your Cosmic Friend.

11

Avoid negative thinking. Remember, whatever you project onto the world will return to you in time, with an inevitable boomerang effect.

12

Respect **everyone**, even those who seem a little daft. For God dwells in all beings, and can express His wisdom through anyone. I have actually found, sometimes, that, if I listened respectfully to someone who seemed to be speaking foolishly, God chose that very person to tell me something I needed to hear.

13

Listen **for expressions** of truth in the simple speech of children. Their insights, being less conditioned by convention, are often refreshingly perceptive. Be careful, however, not to be so unguarded as to create trouble for others. To give an amusing (but illustrative) example, during my family's visit to America when I was nine, my mother took us three boys across the border into Canada. Coming back through customs, the officer asked her, "Have you anything to declare?" "Nothing," she answered. Instantly we all three reacted with dismay. Our hands over our mouths, we cried together, "Oh, Mother!" Sternly the man ordered her to open the car trunk. There he found three little birch-bark canoes, six inches long! So—be childlike, but don't be naive.

February

14

Live more in the heart. Send rays of love outward to all the world, recognizing that all human beings aspire, each in his own way, to the highest possible attainment: supreme bliss. Bliss will come to them eventually, when they achieve perfect union with God.

15

If you lament anything, consider how you'll probably feel a week—a month—a year later. If you can imagine being happy then, why waste all that time? *Be happy now!*

16

Treat others as though it were a treat to be with them!

17

State the truth in normal, conversational tones. People who proclaim their thoughts too loudly are usually lying.

18

Speak the truth kindly—never in a spirit of judgment, and never sarcastically. Speak it in order to be helpful, never to destroy a person's self-image.

19

When setting out to accomplish anything, give less thought to what has already been done than to what is required by this particular task, at this particular time.

20

Be patient with people. Remember, it takes incarnations to climb out of the yawning chasm of delusion. Think how long it may have taken *you* to reach your present level of understanding, and how long it has taken, sometimes, to overcome even one serious flaw.

21

Encourage others in any effort they make to improve themselves. But remember, *they don't owe it to you* to be better than they are. The debt they owe is to themselves alone.

February

22

Bring peace to your own heart first, then send it out as rays of harmony to all the world. The more you radiate peace and harmony to others, the more you will find yourself protected from all harm.

23

Think of this day as a friend. God gave it to you, and wants you to be happy in it. If it rains, tell yourself, "God is seeking, through this shower, to cleanse me of all impurities." And when the sun shines, see its luminescence as God's encouragement to you to do your best.

24

State your opinions impersonally, and not loudly, lest you draw people's attention more to yourself than to your ideas.

25

Treat your friends as though you had much to learn from them. There is no surer way of losing a friend than to make him feel you want or need nothing from him, and that he has nothing to give you.

26

When teaching or advising others, feel that you are *sharing* with them your ideas, knowledge, and experience. Never be didactic or condescending toward anyone.

27

To overcome nervousness while teaching or lecturing, see yourself as *giving out* to others, not desiring that they have a good impression of you.

28

To overcome fear of misjudgment by others, think of them kindly, and also speak to them kindly. Your fears will then be transformed from self-concern into an expansive concern for the well-being of all.

February

29

A **key to introspection** is to focus on the rhythms of your breath: on its calmness or rapidity; on its force of flow; on the location of that flow in the nostrils; on the pauses between the breaths; on the duration of inhalation relative to exhalation. (In sleep, for instance, one's exhalation is twice as long as the inhalation.) Your breathing reflects your mental state. As you watch the breath, you will become inwardly calm.

March

March

1

View life as a mountain to be climbed, every upward move bringing you closer to the top and to perfection. Welcome the difficulties on the way; you will gain strength from facing them. Concentrate on what you must do today, to reach the goal.

2

Act without desire for the fruits of your action. Take care of the present, and the future will take care of itself. The past will cease, then, to burden your conscience, and the future will await you with a smile.

3

After every deed, pause awhile to enjoy your true Self. Effective action always proceeds from a sense of inner peace.

4

Respect others, and they'll always respect you. Despise them, and they'll find many ways to look on you with contempt.

March

5

If you want loyalty from others, give loyalty to them first. Loyalty, like a rudder, holds the barque of life true to its course.

6

More important even than love are respect and loyalty. In love there may be attachment and desire, but in respect, as in loyalty, there is only self-giving.

7

Gaze into the sun when it is near the horizon (its rays will not harm your eyes then). God, through the sun, sends rays of power, endurance, and wisdom. In India, certain meditators practice gazing into the sun, and actually, thereby, receive enlightenment.

8

Gaze into the moon, especially when it is full. Feel in its rays the Divine Mother's eternal love for you and for all Her human children.

Do It *Well!*

9

Listen as much to the tone of people's voices as to their words. *How* they speak is often more important than what they say.

10

If someone tells lies about you, respond calmly and with dignity. If a comment is demanded of you, you might say, "This time my critic has missed the mark, but is it an issue that I'm not perfect? The perfection I am truly seeking is something I wish also for everyone."

11

Be courteous equally to friends and strangers. Courtesy to strangers will win their cooperation and respect. Courtesy to friends will maintain that slight space between you which keeps friendship ever fresh, alive, and interesting.

March

12

Hold kindness in your heart for everyone. Blame no one for his mistakes. Reflect that all are seeking, each in his own way, escape from the dense jungle of delusion.

13

How should you respond to a false accusation? You might try answering, "Now that you've reduced me to a level you can handle, may we talk as friends?" (That subtle reprimand will be well deserved!)

14

Respond to rudeness with courtesy. You might even say with a smile, "Life is all the richer for the many points of view it presents."

15

Treat every difference of opinion with respect. You may then find agreement between what seemed at first to be conflicting points of view.

16

Be honest and truthful even when threatened by disaster, and you will do more than survive: you will flourish.

17

Try always to relate to what *is*, not to what you wish were so.

18

Trust life, even if you cannot trust everybody. Human nature is unreliable, but life is ruled by Immutable Law, and right action will always win in the end.

19

To find inner freedom, live to serve others, not to gain or benefit from them. Service is magnanimity: the prerogative of kings. To desire personal gain is to beggar yourself.

March

20

The more you share with others, the more you will receive the blessing of abundance.

21

In reply to those who speak against you, say, "Thank you. You've helped me affirm that which alone is real to me: the joy of my inner being." A "friend" once spent a whole hour sternly denouncing me for my faults as he saw them; they seemed in some way to disturb his peace of mind. I thanked him, but said nothing more. After he'd left me, however, I wrote what may now be one of my best songs: "Though green summer fade and winter draw near, my Lord, in Your presence I live without fear." I am forever grateful to my caustic critic.

22

Today, make it a point to laugh at least three times from your heart. Heartfelt laughter is the strongest antidote for disease, depression, and corroding desires of every kind.

March

23

Try to understand points of view that are not your own. The mind, like the body, must be stretched now and then, to keep it limber. Otherwise, it may ossify.

24

When bargaining, seek benefits that are mutual. If you are generous in this way, you will usually receive fair treatment in return.

25

Never impose your ideas on anyone. *Offer* them, instead, as kindly suggestions, or as thoughts for consideration. You will find, then, that whatever you say will be more readily accepted.

26

Life demands of us many compromises. Make sure only that you adapt the compromises to your principles, and never your principles to any compromise.

March

27

Criticize no one. If you must correct someone, give him the means also to preserve his self-respect. If you support others, they will support you. If you let people know you are on their side, they will side with you when you most need it.

28

Counting to ten is a known technique for dissipating anger. I suggest taking it a step further: Visualize with each number you count a progressive expansion of consciousness. In thus incrementally broadening your perspective, your anger will be dissipated, and be changed, first to acceptance, then to empathy.

29

Don't try to impress others with how clever you are. Win them, rather, by your sincerity.

30

Today, **treat as your friend** a neighbor you hardly know. Ask him if there is anything you might do to make your proximity of residence more pleasing to him. By your good will, contradict the ancient dictum, "Your neighbor is your enemy; your neighbor's neighbor is your friend."

31

Think **of life as dancing** on air. Soar up lightly in spirit over every mountain of difficulty, on gossamer wings of pure joy.

April

April

1

Humor may be described as arising from a sudden release of tension, introduced by some unexpected incongruity. The incongruity, if not released, may approximate hysteria.* From a release of tension, however, there follows an *upward* relaxation into the higher Self, resulting in glimpses of soul joy. Let this year's "April Fool's Day" bring you inner happiness, not outward mockery.

2

Be generous in victory. It will entail *self*-conquest if it brings you, not pride, but a deep sense of gratitude.

3

Welcome suggestions for improving on your ideas. At the same time, protect your thoughts from too much meddling on the part of others. Be very clear in your own mind as to your true intentions.

---

*   For students of yoga, an imbalance and confusion between the *iḍa* and *pingala* nerve channels.

April

4

If you have a good idea, it may be wise to speak of it only to those who share your ideals, but to protect it from those who might jeer at it because it doesn't conform to their own preconceptions. Let your inspiration grow strong before you expose it to human goats who love to nibble on the inspirations of others.

5

To achieve inner freedom, make a bonfire every night, before going to sleep, of all your attachments, self-definitions, desires, and aversions. Nothing that can be measured, weighed, timed, or physically treasured is truly yours. Toss into the flames, piece by piece, every mental burden. Offer thanks to heaven as your limitations go up in smoke.

6

Attachments are self-limiting. Each one is a prison bar, enclosing you. Ah, but see! Though the bars confine you, there is still space between them. If you dwell mentally on that space, the bars will disappear! Their metal is only the iron of your own stubbornness, its atoms cohering by your constant affirmation of a false reality.

7

Make it a point, today, to tell someone dear to you, "I deeply appreciate you for what you *are*, for what you do for others, and for what you have given me."

8

This day, make it a point to single out someone whose worth many people fail to appreciate; take the time to express your own appreciation. He must have *some* admirable quality: emphasize it.

9

Let nothing tempt you to compromise your highest ideals. Morality is not a question of social mores. The Ten Commandments are engraved in human nature on tablets of light. It is wrong to murder or to steal because it most hurts the perpetrator himself, enclosing him more and more firmly within the rock walls of egoism. Armed with truthfulness, honesty, and integrity, however, you will always win in the end.

10

Purity, innocence, and an absence of selfish motive: These, together, form a diadem more brilliant than any that ever graced emperor's brow.

11

Tune in to the personal realities of those to whom, or with whom, you speak. Though the words you use be similar, your realities may be almost as varied as different languages.

April

12

Be more concerned with understanding others than with being understood by them. In this way, they'll usually give you their wholehearted support.

13

Be happy in yourself. If you hold out a begging bowl to life, as if pleading for happiness, you'll find the bowl always empty.

14

Be "solution-oriented," not "problem-oriented." Problem-consciousness only draws more problems to itself, even as flypaper draws flies. Solution-consciousness, however, attracts solutions like a magnet, unraveling every problem, and showing the way out of every difficulty.

April

15

Don't confuse cleverness with intelligence. True intelligence is not only cerebral. To be fully conscious, there must be also both feeling and some sense of *personal* involvement. Cleverness usually indicates diminished feeling, and an attempt at non-involvement.

16

See every problem as an opportunity. Each time you face a problem and overcome it, your supply of energy will increase.

17

Be ever restful in your heart. A restful spirit will help you more quickly than weeks of fretful talking or pondering on your difficulties.

18

Speak kindly to animals. As a human being can be uplifted by the thought of, or mental association with, angels, animals, similarly, are hastened in their evolution by association with human beings. You yourself will be helped also, if you extend to animals a helping hand.

19

Seek upliftment in the company you keep. The magnetism your associates possess will affect your state of consciousness for either good or evil. Make it a point, therefore, to seek out the company of those whose qualities you want to develop in yourself. This is the chief benefit of living in spiritual community with others of like mind.

20

Gaze into the eyes of others, if you want to attract their magnetism. Avoid doing so, however, if you think their magnetism might prove harmful to you. And if your aim in life really is to "do it well," as the title of this book proclaims, try to emerge from the lowlands of delusion, where swamps of ignorance breed sufferings of every kind. It is important, in the fulfillment of this aim, to avoid contact with anyone who might drag you down again. Any state of consciousness that can keep people wallowing in delusion for incarnations must have some magnetism of its own; the truth seeker must avoid such an influence as he would a contagious disease. Avoid especially gazing into the eyes of people who live only to gratify their senses.

21

When eating, be either alone or in uplifting company. For when one is eating, he places himself in an absorbing mode, with the result that he is more open to the vibrations in his vicinity. In restaurants, or in any public eating place that emanates heterogeneous vibrations, make it a point to be centered more than usually in yourself. Otherwise, if you must go to such places, go with true friends. Always eat in harmony.

22

In the vibratory interchange between the sexes, there exists a strong magnetism. Maintain a discreet mental distance, therefore, especially from members of the other sex whose consciousness is worldly. Minimize contact, especially of the eyes and hands. (A handclasp creates two horseshoe magnets: the one upward, uniting the two upper bodies; the other downward, uniting the lower bodies.) At such times especially, be centered within.

23

In any magnetic interchange, what you give out will affect what you receive. For the greatest protection, think of yourself as channeling God's power.

24

A **principle of** magnetic interchange between people is that the stronger magnet always influences the weaker, never the reverse. Unless you possess great inner strength, therefore, never think you have the power to uplift everyone by the mere exercise of good will. (A good illustration of this point may be found in Somerset Maugham's short story, "Rain.")

25

Keep a spiritual bodyguard, when circumstances require you to mix with spiritually uncongenial people. The magnetism of two is stronger than that of one. When moving in a crowd, try never to go alone. But if you must do so, imagine yourself enveloped in a cloak of light.

26

Be **always grateful**—to others, to life, to God. Express appreciation to life for everything. Appreciation and gratitude, even for such a test as deep suffering, will attract to you an abundance of blessings.

April

27

Let others feel your support in their worthwhile enterprises. Even if you don't approve of something they do, let them feel your support for what they *are*.

28

To break a person's will is sinful before God. Allow others to develop at their own pace, make their own mistakes, and learn their own lessons. Otherwise, they will never grow.

29

Sow seeds of faith, where others have sown doubt.

30

Don't ask more of others than you would ask of yourself.

May

May

1

There are two kinds of innocence: one, of ignorance, and the other, of wisdom. A little girl, asked once by a little boy, "Are you a virgin?" replied, "No, not yet." Hers was the innocence of ignorance. Such innocence may in time be undermined. The innocence of wisdom, however, entails the complete conquest of ego. Such innocence, though childlike, can never be corrupted or destroyed. Its strength, though flexible, is indomitable.

2

Sound and light affect our consciousness, for we, like them, are composed of vibrations. Music, therefore, is not mere entertainment, and lighting is not merely something by which to read. Both sound and light actually affect your consciousness, helping to mold it toward either spiritual nobility, or toward worldliness and depravity. Be sensitive to the subtle effect of whatever vibrations there are around you, and protect yourself from the disruptive ones by listening to music that inspires, or by singing (even mentally) uplifting songs, and by surrounding yourself with soothing lights and colors.

May

3

Select music for its melody, rhythm, and harmony. A melody does more than entertain: it can uplift, or depress. A rhythm can either calm the nerves, stimulate them positively, or agitate and distress them. Harmony can evoke deep feelings—whether of love and happiness, or of anger, depression—loneliness. Choose your music wisely, for it can deeply affect your state of consciousness.

4

The colors of the rainbow are not only primary sensorily: they also have an effect on your consciousness. They resonate with your aura—the field of energy you project around you. Surround yourself with pure colors. Muddy colors may lessen your mental clarity. Brighter shades can induce brighter emotions. Choose carefully. Colors should resonate with your nature as it is, and with that which you would like to develop.

5

The color red can be cheerful. It can also—especially if muddy—inflame to lust or anger. If red resonates with you, make sure that it stimulates you in the right way—helping to make you cheerful, bright, and happy.

6

The color orange reminds one of fire. It can help to awaken in you an enthusiasm for burning away all obstacles and difficulties. On the other hand, orange can also irritate, especially if your nature tends toward a too placid serenity.

7

Yellow is the color of wisdom, insight, and calm acceptance. It can disturb you, however, if you resist challenges. If what you seek is progress, yellow can help to make you more creative. An impure yellow can have a sickening effect on the mind.

May

8

Green is the color of health and harmony; it is the color most visible among growing things. It gives a heightened sense of physical and mental well-being. Where there is health, however, there can also be ill health. Unpleasant shades of green can disturb the emotions. Therefore this color is often associated with harmful emotions also, such as envy and jealousy.

9

Blue is the color of expansive calmness. Without warmth, however, blue can withhold the feeling quality. (Consider the term, "steely blue.") This color, therefore, should contain a certain richness. Its influence should be uplifting and calmly devotional. Blue is a good color for meditation.

10

Indigo implies rich, pure feeling, and the love of beauty in all its manifestations. Choose indigo to help deepen your love for others, and appreciation for the goodness in them and in all life. Indigo in its negative aspects, however, especially for those whose feeling quality takes them down the spine, generates attitudes of rejection.

Do It *Well!*

May

11

Violet is the color of high thoughts, high principles, noble aspirations. This color will help to lift you out of the baser feelings into the realization that you, in your true Self, are pure Spirit. Violet in its negative aspects can erect a psychic wall between yourself and the earthy realities around you, making your ideals unrealistic and impractical.

12

White is a blend of all the colors of the rainbow. It can infuse an attitude of either purity or disinterest, depending on whether your energy moves up toward the brain, or withdraws into the spine passively. Choose white to develop non-attachment and non-involvement with the world. Don't choose it if your nature is too blandly passive.

May

13

Ideas should be presented with simple, grounding examples. Don't offer people mere abstractions. The more specific you are, the clearer will be your own thoughts, and the clearer also the understanding you convey. When describing waves in their relation to the ocean, for example, see and hear those waves clearly in your mind. Such clear visualization will help to make your description more vivid.

14

True happiness is not the fruit of years of painful struggle and anxiety. It is a long succession of little decisions simply to *be* happy in the moment. As my Guru said, "The minutes are more important than the years."

15

Accept adversity calmly. It is intrinsic to the cosmic drama. Indeed, without tension there would *be* no drama. The greatest adversities can be turned to advantage, once we accept them calmly.

16

Eat a balanced diet. A good formula for doing so is to select foods of varied colors: the deeper the colors, the richer the food content.

17

Make inner freedom your chief goal in life. Think of the many desires and attachments that hold you down as being like ropes on a balloon, tying it to the ground. Cut those ropes one by one, exclaiming vigorously as you do so, "You can hold me no longer! My true place is high in the sky, soaring over seas and continents, wafted on winds of pure bliss."

18

When presenting your ideas to others, illustrate them with familiar examples. The more familiar the image, the sharper the understanding you'll convey. For example, children are often told the pleasant myth that there is, at the end of every rainbow, a pot of gold. Usually one thinks of a rainbow as high up in the sky, or at any rate far away. Suggest rather, then, a test of this myth closer to hand: the rainbow which appears in the mist formed by a garden sprinkler. Could there really be gold at the end of that little spray? One can always dig there, and see.

19

Every time you inhale, think you are inhaling energy. *Pranayama*, a yoga practice, means not only "breath control," but "control of the energy." In filling your lungs, feel your entire being—body, mind, feelings, aspirations—filling with energy and joy.

20

Advice for men: If you maintain a certain reserve in the presence of women, they will always respect you.

May

21

Advice for women: There are two ways to relate to men. If you flirt with them or try to tempt them, you may win them easily; doing so will give you a sense of power over them. That power, however, will be delusive. Subconsciously, they will resent you for drawing on their energy, even though they won't always understand the reason for their resentment. If, however, you behave toward men more givingly, as a mother or a friend, you will *give* them energy, and they will always appreciate you. This is why women, in India, are spoken of as men's *shakti* (strength, or energy). As temptresses, however, they are not *shakti*, but *ashakti*.

22

Advice, **again**, **for men**: It is easier for you to be impersonal. Dwell more, therefore, on the thought of infinity, of freedom from ego, and of the well-being of all. Let your search for God be for His Bliss, even more than for His love. Think in terms of expansive service to God, through others.

May

23

Further advice for women: Because it comes more naturally to you to be personal, concentrate on developing an intimate, I-and-Thou relationship with God. Serve Him in personal ways. Keep a beautiful altar; surround yourself with sweet, spiritual images. Enjoy all the beauties of Nature in God's name.

24

Advice to men on the subject of balance: As men progress spiritually, they take on certain feminine characteristics: becoming softer, gentler, more considerate of the needs of others, more receptive, and readier to listen to what others have to say (all these being signs of feminine maturity, though not evident in all women!). The reason breasts are attractive is that they at least *suggest* tenderness of heart. Physically speaking men too may for this reason develop slight breasts. It may be difficult for men at this point to control their feelings of tenderness; thus, they may weep easily.

25

Advice to women who seek balance: As you progress spiritually, your feminine nature will become balanced by masculine characteristics. You may become more affirmative, less personal, firmer in your walk, more outward in your self-expression—as if your energy were drawn more naturally to the point between the eyebrows, making your every gesture more decisive.

26

In balance: The attraction that exists naturally between the sexes ceases to be compelling, and becomes merely a matter of interest. Men cease to feel obliterated by women (notice how often men are silent at parties, in the company of women). Women cease to feel bullied by men. Men cease, in a positive way, to feel tenderly protective of women, and women cease to depend on men for protection. Both sexes then appear to each other as human beings, simply, equal in worth like the two sides of a coin.

May

27

Think how many kinds of laughter there are! The "belly laughs" which proceed from excessive body- and matter-consciousness. Laughs that emanate from the cervical center behind the throat, conveying a sense of calmness. Laughs that originate in the medulla oblongata at the base of the brain, and refer constantly back to the ego. Laughs that originate from the Christ center between the eyebrows, and, when their energy sinks back toward the medulla, are negative and deprecatory, but if the energy flows forward, are positive, indicating discrimination. Laughs that proceed from energy descending in the spine from the heart tend always to be cynical, sarcastic, or bitter. The best laugh of all is one that directs kindly energy upward from the heart to the Christ center in the forehead.

28

Don't joke too much, lest in so doing you trivialize your relationships. Controlled merriment helps in releasing tensions, but uncontrolled jocularity keeps the mind light, and prevents one from exercising deep thought.

29

Live more within yourself. Always remain a little reserved, even when laughing. Be soft-spoken, respectful, and appreciative of everyone and everything. When you are by yourself, be withdrawn inwardly.

30

If someone criticizes you, answer him, "I appreciate your taking the trouble to offer me advice, and I will think about it." In this way, you will not necessarily be saying you agree with him, but will show that you are open to improvement, and are not defensive. At the same time, don't place yourself under obligation to accept advice from anyone.

31

Forgive others, and life itself will forgive you. The karmic blows you attract will be deflected by the bright, protective aura with which forgiveness surrounds you. And your karma itself, then, will emanate softer rays.

June

June

1

Accept others as they are, and you'll attract supportive friends wherever you go.

2

Speak the truth always—kindly, and impersonally. Truth is ever beneficial. To tell someone he is ugly or stupid would be of no benefit to him; speak only the helpful truth. The gift of silence, for one who would be truthful, is essential. Truthfulness requires that one weigh his words before giving them utterance.

3

Truthfulness requires an acceptance of things as they are. Wishful thinking leads to wishful talking, which can bend perceptions to suit one's own, or other people's, mere fancy.

June

4

Say what you mean; then stop. Think of commas on a page, which look like distorted periods. As a comma is used, often unnaturally, to extend the thoughts in a sentence, so do many people drag their thoughts out unnecessarily. In writing, in conversation, and very much so in public speaking, it is important to be clear, succinct, and *satisfied* with sufficiency.

5

The way you *end* a thought, a sentence, or a paragraph is important. Many people, when speaking or reading, lower their voices at the end of a thought. Many writers trail off similarly, and end not with a key word, but weakly, as if suddenly doubtful of what promised to be convincing. In a lecture, this tendency to peter out at the end of sentences may be due only to loss of breath, but even with that excuse it is a poor way to present one's thoughts. End with a flourish! End with a "punch line." End each sentence on a note of power. In classical drama, the climax at the end of a play is followed by a brief anticlimax. Good! The anticlimax gives the viewer time at the end to relax and absorb what he has experienced. Building to that climax, however, requires a gradual increase of tension, not an increase of anticlimaxes.

June

6

Speak the truth always, and Nature itself will support you in every undertaking.

7

Present the truth interestingly. Many people think that to be truthful means to be dull and "matter of fact." Bliss is never dull, however, and bliss is the reality underlying all of Cosmic Creation! Often, truth and fact are, in this respect, very different realities! Align the truths you speak with the bliss of the universe.

June

8

Sometimes a fact may contradict a truth. To call someone evil may describe his behavior factually, but it cannot describe what he *is* in his soul. Nor does it describe his potential for spiritual greatness, something which all human beings possess. That tangle of vegetation you see floating down the river soon passes out of sight. All people are moving—some of them in the wrong direction, but eventually and however windingly toward Bliss in God. If you fail in some attempt to reach a worthwhile goal, never say, "I have failed." Say rather, "I have not yet succeeded!" Yesterday, did you err? Then say, "I erred. But I *will* win through." With that attitude, you *cannot but succeed* in the end.

9

Cling firmly to your ideals, even when weakness pulls you repeatedly into delusion. *You are not your mistakes!*

June

10

Honor your commitments, even those you make to yourself. If you've told someone, "I'll go out and buy a newspaper today," and the news you wanted then reaches you by some other means, go out and buy the paper anyway. Do so purely to maintain your promise—to him, and to yourself. For you should view even casual commitments in the light of promises. To do so will give you such a power of truth that your mere word will have materializing power, backed by cosmic truth itself.

11

Always keep your spine straight. The spine is the channel through which energy flows up to the brain. If that flow becomes weak, your power to meet life's challenges will decrease. Truthfulness demands a straightforward attitude: firmness, integrity, and clear vision. All these virtues depend on a clear upward flow of energy to the brain.

12

Look straight into people's eyes—not in daring as liars often do who look *at*, but not *into*, people's eyes—but with a desire to include others in your thoughts and feelings.

June

13

To be true to others means being loyal to them. Truth and loyalty are virtual synonyms. Therefore my Guru said, "Loyalty is the first law of God." Indeed, disloyalty is worse than untruthfulness, for weak character may force a person to be untruthful, but in treachery there is no such compulsion: there is simply egoic attachment to delusion.

14

Acceptance is the first secret of overcoming heartbreak and disappointment. Suffering always arises from wishing that things were other than they are.

15

Heartbreak can be overcome by offering oneself up to God. In this realm of duality, life brings constant disappointments. Only in God is perfect bliss attainable. Accept pain as a reminder of that truth, and as a corrective to any wrong directions in your life. If you live wholeheartedly for God, pain will keep you on the narrow path which leads to Him.

16

Be grateful for disappointments! Give them to God, and you will find them always, in the end, to have been the best thing that could have happened to you. Disappointments are God's way of opening up for you new windows of opportunity.

17

"**T**here are no such things** as obstacles: there are only opportunities!" This teaching of my Guru's might well be engraved over the exit of every home. Obstacles summon us to put forth greater energy. Without them, people would sink into lethargy. Indeed, even the worst karma is a blessing: a goad to improve oneself.

18

If people disappoint you, never turn against them. Accept the disappointment as a karmic lesson, and tell God firmly, "No matter how many storms of life howl around me, how heavily the rains fall, how mightily the earth shakes, or how violently circumstances pummel and punish me, I am Thine, ever Thine! Thou art my only truth, my only reality in this world!" For your own sake if for no one else's, keep a soft and ever kindly heart. By anger and bitterness you will only hurt yourself.

19

Direct every sorrow upward from your heart to the Christ center between the eyebrows. The more determinedly you raise your consciousness, the closer you will come to understanding that grief is but a delusion, born of egoic separation from your true Self, God.

June

20

Bathe your heart's sorrows with the holy, purifying water of devotion. Look upon sorrow as mere dirt—something to be washed away by an intense flow of devotional love, the *direction* of that flow being ever upward, toward union with your Divine Beloved.

21

Moods, griefs, and sorrows of every kind cannot be reasoned away. They have their own reality, and exert their own power. The only cure for them is to change your level of consciousness. When I was young, I used to drive moods and faults away by concentrating—once, even fiercely—at the point between the eyebrows.

22

Feel the wind on your skin. Ask yourself, "Whence comes this breath of air? Where, after leaving me, will it go?" Let every breeze heighten your awareness of other places, other times, other realities.

 June

23

Make **communication** with others an exchange of vibrations, not only of ideas.

24

If **you want to enjoy** life, take yourself less seriously.

25

To **overcome** the temptation to tell tales on others, tell good ones on yourself.

26

Live *in*, **but not** *for*, the present moment. In that way you will affirm your timeless, spaceless reality.

27

Be **good-humored** about the shortcomings of others, and you'll find it easier to handle shortcomings in yourself. Remember, your faults can be either overwhelming or insignificant, depending only on what imagination makes of them.

June

28

Give others credit, where possible, in the anecdotes you tell. Not only will they appreciate being included, but you'll lessen the grip your own ego (the cause of all your misfortunes) has on you.

29

To develop concentration, do one thing at a time, and *do it well!*

30

Accept criticism impartially. Remember, whatever is simply *is*; and what is not cannot be spoken into existence. Truth, in all things, is the final arbiter.

July

July

1

Encourage good ideas, no matter what their source.

2

Depend on nothing outside yourself. Free yourself inwardly by letting no outer circumstance condition your happiness. If a desire arises in your mind and causes you to imagine something outward making you happy, offer up the desire to God in the complete certainty, born of humanity's long experience, that in Him alone does true happiness lie.

July

3

Make contentment your criterion of prosperity. Wealth is primarily the *consciousness* of abundance. And poverty is the *consciousness* of lack. You can be rich though dressed in a loincloth and living under a tree. And you can be poor though residing proudly in a mansion, served by bustling servants, surrounded by rich furnishings, and possessing a bank account running to many millions. A criterion of true wealth is also indifference to the mere opinions of others. Only by the yardstick of inner happiness can you tell how rich you truly are. If you are burdened with an excess of luxury and held a prisoner to the expectations of others, you will pass life indeed in a state of misery.

Do It *Well!*

4

Independence Day in America: The political and national freedom celebrated this day were supposed to give all men a chance to rise to their own highest potential. Independence was meant to be applied directionally; it has taken time for blacks and for women to be granted the right to vote, though it should always have been seen as their right. The time has arrived for another freedom to be declared: freedom of conscience. This declaration can be made only by and for oneself. Let no one pressure you into thinking and behaving as *they* think you should. God has a special song to sing through you, one which you alone can offer to the world.

July

5

My bottom line for many years has been, not money or profit of any kind, but inner peace. I've refused to allow myself to become so stressed as to sacrifice that treasure. It is better, I've felt—and experience has borne me out—to leave undone even important things, if attention to them might undermine my peace. For without peace, I would be all too prone to error. From inner peace, moreover, come enlightened decisions. People's expectations of me can never equal what is expected of me by God: my peace in the thought of Him.

6

If someone accuses you of something you did in the past, say, "What matters is not what happened in the past, but what I am now." If you have changed, say so. But if the accusation is invalid, the question of change doesn't arise. If your accuser is right, and you have still to change enough, reply instead, "Is anyone perfect? And do you think I need your permission to clean my own laundry?" To finish the thought, even if your accuser is mistaken in every way, you might say to him, "I am what I am before my conscience and God." In this way, you will refrain from lowering yourself to a level of self-justification or counter-accusation. If, on the other hand, your accuser has been actually vicious, you might reply to him, "Do your own laundry!"

7

Let no one pressure you with his opinions. Be guided from within. My own family did their best to get me to forsake my spiritual calling. I am glad to say I adamantly rejected their every plea. I had my own star to follow, and it has led me to inner peace. Their wishes, on the other hand, would have resulted in my lasting sorrow, disappointment, and frustration. Therefore I say, *Follow your own star!*

8

Let no one agitate you. If you lose your peace, you will never know happiness. If ever you do feel agitated, calm your heart's feelings. Let your reactions spring from within yourself. Let no one impose on you his hopes, desires, or expectations. Even if you are placed behind prison bars, no one will be able to imprison your mind. Personal integrity is the first essential for soul-liberation.

 *July*

9

If your cause is just, don't be afraid to disappoint others. See to it only that you never disappoint God.

10

Be firmly loyal to your principles, but never demand of others that they share those principles with you. Respect their right to seek wisdom in their own way, and at their own pace.

11

Isn't it interesting, how people's tendency is to shout when they meet after long separation! Why all that noise? We might compare it to starting a car: first comes a high sound to get the car moving. A low, steady hum follows when the desired speed has been reached. And note the low growl of the motor as it is shut off. It is like the three aspects of AUM, the Cosmic Vibration of the universe: Brahma, the Creator (a relatively high sound); Vishnu, the Preserver (a medium sound); and Shiva, the All-Dissolver (the lowest sound). Contrasted to first meetings, partings often end on a lower note—sometimes of regret at the fact of parting; sometimes, if the meeting lacked energy, emitting a dismissive note. To keep a reunion with friends fresh and interesting, focus especially on the medium—the Vishnu—aspect, by giving to your reunion even more than you receive from it. "Fuel" your conversation with inner happiness.

12

Make everyone feel that he or she is special in your eyes—not in any particular way, necessarily, but above all because every human being is your brother or sister, in God.

13

Be expansive in your sympathies. Don't limit them to thoughts of "I" and "mine." All men are God's children; so too are you. Don't be a stranger to anyone. The sorrows and joys of all mankind are, though in different ways, your own.

July

14

Most of the pains we experience, whether physically or mentally, are painful only because we so define them. Think of those pains as events, merely, of only minimal concern to you. Remove yourself mentally from all outer experiences, and you'll gain the ability to bear pain and suffering easily.

15

Regardless of how people treat you, determine your response to them by the criterion of inner freedom. How others behave toward you is their business; how *you* respond to them is yours. Suppose someone tells you he hates you: Will it make you happier by, in return, hating him? It will be more in your own interest to offer him, instead, your sincere friendship.

16

Is there any subject on which you feel sensitive? If so, decide, "I will change myself." A sore spot on the body tells us something is wrong there. When people "rub you the wrong way," see what is wrong in yourself that you've been made to flinch.

Do It *Well!*

July

17

When an elder or a superior takes you to task, listen impersonally, but don't tell yourself, "That person *must* be right. Look at the position he holds!" People are people, each with his own faults and weaknesses, which often stick to him like burrs until he achieves enlightenment. Indeed, spiritual development, like sunlight pouring through a stained-glass window, may actually highlight a person's flaws, until further spiritual progress eliminates his ego altogether.

18

Judge a person (if you must) not by his foibles, but by how sincerely he is seeking truth and God. The less you judge others, the better you will be able to accept yourself as you are. Self-acceptance, moreover, is the first step to self-correction. Remember my Guru's words: "God doesn't mind your faults: He minds your indifference."

July

19

How can one love everyone on earth? Here's an easy way: Reflect that God's nature is, as scripture declares, *Satchidananda*: ever-existing, ever-conscious, ever-new Bliss. It is He, the Creator, who gives each of us our basic motivation. The eternal motive behind every action, therefore, is our need to unravel the secret of existence as perfect bliss. Even the worst criminal seeks the same bliss as does every saint. The crook seeks bliss mistakenly, of course; yet he does so unmistakably. Everyone on earth hungers for that highest fulfillment, no matter how indirect his method of seeking it. Isn't this reason enough to love, and be compassionate toward, everyone on earth?

20

To overcome a judgmental attitude in yourself, observe others who have similar attitudes. Are they not projecting outward, merely, an insecurity in themselves? In judging others you only judge yourself. Offer kind acceptance to everyone. Doing so will not only deepen your faith in God: it will give you deeper faith in your own potential.

July

21

Encourage others, if you would inwardly feel God's encouragement, in your heart.

22

Self-knowledge gives a deeper understanding of others. Though some believe what they want is money, or fame, or power, or pleasure, or material success, their motivation is essentially always the same: in their hearts they are driven by the universal longing for bliss. This subtle truth links all beings together in one cosmic family. The deeper you go in self-understanding, the more completely you will understand everyone. You can even, if you so desire, acquire their skills and traits. In this way, you can develop any ability.

23

When going anywhere as a tourist, don't be satisfied with merely "seeing the sights." Try to feel the vibrations of places. You will find, in time, that you can actually feel some of the history of those places, and the consciousness of people who lived there long ago. A Mexican friend of mine from Yucatán once described to me a very clear vision he'd had of an ancient temple complex. He saw the old Mayans passing in and out, as though they still lived there. Everything you see around you is composed of consciousness, which emits vibrations, which in turn endure for centuries—perhaps even forever.

24

When others project disharmony, send out to them in return rays of harmonious energy from your heart. The more consciously you bless them, the more they will change. In time, they too will project harmony.

July

25

Why is there so much violence in the world? Surely it is because people are disharmonious *in themselves.* Today's terrorists imagine they'll improve the world by making it over in their own image. Were they ever to succeed, however, in killing everyone who disagreed with them, they'd only turn their energies to butchering one another. Ultimately, the only way for the world to know peace is for people everywhere to seek it within themselves.

26

Meet anger, when possible, with the soothing touch of silence, respect, and good will. Don't let another's anger shake you from that intention. It is the way to keep from being sucked, yourself, into another person's beehive of emotion. Only by inward firmness will your influence for good spread, perhaps ultimately including also that other person.

July

27

Never resort to self-justification. If people are interested in hearing your explanation, state the facts simply and impersonally, but never descend, unworthily, to self-defense.

28

To be truly creative, work with an attitude of bliss. God's motive in creating the universe was not only "to enjoy Himself through many," as the Indian scriptures declare, but also that, His nature being bliss, it is the essence of that bliss nature to be self-expansive. Despite widespread suffering on earth, the long, winding tale of every soul has its ending in perfect bliss—a bliss, as Yogananda put it, "beyond imagination of expectancy."

July

29

To inject uplifting vibrations into anything you write, work hard at getting the word-sequences right. A sequence will "work" best if it follows the natural flow of human thought. Read your sentences again and again to make sure they achieve such a flow. Reposition words, phrases, and clauses, as necessary, for increasing clarity. For instance, in an earlier version of a sentence for July 15 in this book, I wrote, "Isn't it in your interest to offer him your sincere friendship in return?" I later changed it to read: "It will be more in your own interest to offer him, instead, your sincere friendship." This change places the most important words, "sincere friendship," at the end, making them linger on in memory. When you do this work for your readers, they will benefit from the vibrations of your consciousness.

30

The first and last words of a sentence are especially important. See that all your sentences begin and end well. The rest, then, should come easily.

July

31

In writing, try as much as possible to avoid repeating too closely even such essential words as *and*, *of*, *the*, and *a*. Interchange these last two with one another from time to time. Try to avoid too close a juxtaposition of words that end similarly—words, for example, that end in "-ly," "-ity," or "-tion." If you do repeat similar sounds, do so deliberately, for effect. Remember of course that every rule can sometimes be broken, depending on the kind of interest you want to awaken in others. Even speed readers, however, will prefer a flow that follows the right word-sequence.

August

August

1

To know God, it is said that one must possess "the simplicity of a child." How, one may wonder — considering the vastness and complexity of the universe — can simplicity be part of any equation involving wisdom? The metaphor itself supplies the answer: A child is simple because, although it observes, it doesn't prejudge. Thus, it lives far more in the present than the average adult, who dwells greatly on thoughts of past or future events. For an adult, the present is more like a bridge spanning those two. Be childlike in the sense of living in — but not *for* — the present. Be childlike, but not childish: not overreacting, that is, to every pain or slight.

2

Intuition is simple because it implies direct perception, and not a careful process of joining thoughts and facts together, like the pieces of a jigsaw puzzle. Ordinary people, as they become knowledgeable, become complex. Learn to approach your problems not by puzzling them through, but by withdrawing into your center. There, offer up every problem to that pristine, central simplicity. Never feel you have your answer until you've achieved a simple sense of rightness in your heart.

3

God's consciousness is center everywhere, circumference nowhere. At the periphery of His consciousness lies nothing at all: He is centered equally in every point of space. In that fact lies the secret of divine simplicity. We can approach that simplicity most nearly by imagining Him as a *Person* who has nothing to defend—nothing to promote: who accepts everything as it is, without rejecting anything; who wants nothing from anyone; who sees everything in relation to its eternal and unchanging reality; who is wholly without self-importance; who never condescends; who waits patiently for us, His creatures, to untangle our psychological kinks and realize that we belong wholly to Him. Such is the nature of Perfect Bliss.

4

God's nature is childlike in the sense that He gives us His love without being in any way conditioned by our feelings toward Him. He wants nothing from us. His unceasing hope is to welcome us into His arms of infinity. He has no ulterior motive. There is nothing He wishes from us. He can never be disappointed in us, for in His unconditional love He wants nothing in return but *our* love, since He is eternally complete in Himself.

5

Imagine the worst thing that could happen to you. Then, still imagining, try to accept it. Relax any feeling of rejection in your heart. If you can bear that, you will be inwardly free. Why not accept, then, whatever comes to you unasked? You cannot avoid death itself, so why fear it? Offer yourself up to it, rather, confident in the knowledge that you, yourself, can never die. (And if you think death will obliterate everything for you, why worry anyway? You won't be able to cling to things after that, so live fully now, while you can.)

6

Say to yourself always, as my Guru taught: "What comes of itself, let it come." After even the greatest disaster, life goes on—if not in this world, then in some other. An attitude of relaxed acceptance toward whatever happens in life will bring you much inner peace and happiness.

7

Relax *upward,* toward the spiritual eye in the forehead. Don't try to *force* your concentration to that point. Think of the spiritual eye, rather, as your natural center of awareness.

8

Invite the participation of others, whenever possible, in any decision you make. The more you involve them, the greater will be their own interest, and the greater their commitment to working with you.

9

In inviting others to participate in decisions that are yours to make, the responsibility for the outcome will be yours also. Allow no one's suggestions to be your excuse for failure. Accept only ideas that resonate with your own intuition. Never feel obligated to accept a suggestion merely because you have asked for it.

10

Enlist support for your suggestions, but weigh any disagreement carefully, and listen to counter-suggestions with an open mind.

August

11

Never **reduce people** in your mind to stereotypes. Everyone is, in his own way, unique. To typecast a person is to judge him. Someone who practiced astrology once told me, "You're the 'lone wolf' type." As a matter of fact, I enjoy people and like to work with them. That woman was distressed, merely, because I didn't agree with *her*. (That, indeed, is my main objection to astrology: it tempts one to squeeze others into little psychological boxes of personal prejudice and predilection.)

12

Give **credit to others** whenever possible, even if an idea was your own. Those who try always to draw praise to themselves soon find themselves forced to carry all the responsibility, also. To succeed at anything, especially anything worthwhile, you will almost always need help from others. Involve them therefore, if possible, even now.

13

Make it a practice, when conversing with people, to look at them between the eyebrows, rather than only in the eyes. To stare too fixedly into someone's eyes may seem an invasion of his privacy. If you look away, however, as if to avoid his eyes, it may look as if you were donning a mask. If you look at the floor or at the ground, people will think you can't wait to get away from them. To look off to the side, or up at the ceiling, indicates that, to ponder a point, you are separating yourself from others; this is something you can do only occasionally without conveying the impression that, for you, your interlocutor hardly exists.

14

What is the best handshake? I've had people lightly extend to me two or three fingers, as if implying they'd rather not touch me at all. Others offer their hands limply, as if wishing to disengage as soon as possible. Others cling to your hand as if they considered you a lifeline. Still others squeeze your hand forcefully as if trying to overpower you. The best handshake is firm, friendly, and tactfully brief—neither too personal nor too impersonal. It leaves the other person the integrity of his own space.

August

15

Notice how quickly the human voice reflects a person's feelings. When he is angry, his voice becomes tight and rigid. When he feels avarice, his voice tends to express itself in a harsh croak. Where there is contempt, the voice carries a certain nasal quality. Where there is self-interest, the voice is often thick and clinging. Where there is indifference, the sound is flat and dismissive. All of these tones, and many others, show the extent to which the voice is a sounding board for one's state of consciousness, and also an affirmation of that state. Listen especially for the soft, rich tone of voice in people who love God. Project outward, through your own voice, tones of kindness, good humor, and generosity. Project devotion to God, above all. The more you focus on letting these qualities vibrate through your voice, the more you will find them deepening within you.

August

16

Speech is naturally melodic. See to it that the melody of your speech be pleasant and attractive. Notice the change in that melody with every shift of mood or feeling. Watch for such changes also in others. Learn to detect in the voice sincerity or insincerity; attitudes of defensiveness, of aggression, of deceit; intolerance, kindness, and loyalty. Perception of these qualities depends more on experience than on any clear definition. Some people can tell a lie so convincingly that even discriminating people may, at first, be fooled. There are also melodies conditioned by a person's environment and upbringing. Take these cadences into account also, to see whether the melody of a person's speech is conditioned or spontaneous.

17

Accents are important indicators of attitude, for they are due to more than the influences of upbringing and environment. Ego has its center in the medulla oblongata at the base of the brain. Tension at that point often draws the head backward, causing one to "look down his nose at others," and to speak with a nasal accent. Tension in the medullary region can also make one toss his head back and forth arrogantly. Aggressive will power causes one to force his words out in such a way as to emphasize his consonants. An appeal to people's kinder emotions will soften the consonants, and give emphasis to vowel sounds. Sounds like *ü* and *ö*, though common in certain languages, also suggest, by tightening the lips, an attitude of reluctance. Consonants in which the *h* is pronounced in conjunction with *b*, *p*, *t*, and *k* (such as the Bengali *bhalo* [good]) are also pronounced similarly in all languages when a sentiment is expressed explosively. The American flat *a* is a soft, double sound, as in "man" ("ma-uhn," in which the second sound is almost inaudible); it sounds sweeter than the same word spoken with an English accent. The *r* in the word, "better," sounds warmer and more welcoming in American English than in the Englishman's "bettah." The American double "*t*," on the other hand, sounds muddier and less precise than the English: the American, "bedder"; the English, "better."

18

Humility is not self-deprecation. It is the simple recognition that God alone, in everything, is the Doer. For He acts through instruments. Humility is an important step toward overcoming the sense of "I" and "mine." In humility, however, there remains the sense of an ego opening itself to higher wisdom and guidance. When egolessness is attained, even humility ceases to exist. One's little self is simply no longer a consideration.

19

If it ever becomes your duty in life to form a committee, see that every member has his own area of responsibility. Much time will be saved if you exclude people who, having nothing specific to do, would otherwise talk lengthily and to little purpose just to show their involvement in what is going on. Chat sessions are different, of course, but when there is work to be done, each member should have an area of focus for which he is personally responsible. Thus, when a decision is reached, it can be given to him to implement directly.

August

20

When giving a gift, think not only whether it is something your friend would enjoy receiving, but also whether *you* would enjoy giving it to him. For gifts should carry vibrations of love and happiness. To give someone a painting that he likes, but that you yourself consider an outrage, would deprive the giving of its essential ingredient: joy.

21

Pretend to yourself that this day is the beginning of a new incarnation. Obviously you are not a newborn baby, but try to wipe out any power the past has to keep you doing the same things, making the same mistakes, and performing always in the same old ways. Look for new things to accomplish, new worlds to conquer, new ideas to express. Don't be like those people who declare pompously, "Well, as I always say...." Try to be ever-new in yourself, and in your relations with friends, loved ones, and even strangers.

August

22

Today, tell yourself, "I'm going to see life afresh! When I look at a tree, I will ask myself, 'What message does it have for me, from God?' If its trunk is straight, I'll think, 'That is how I shall keep my spine: ever straight and erect.' If the tree has many branches, I'll think, 'Into what new branch of thought and activity can I grow today?' If the leaves are luxurious, I'll think, 'Let my own life flourish similarly!' And if the tree is bare, let me think, perhaps at first negatively, 'I don't want my life to be barren!' but then positively, 'I, too, must withdraw sometimes from outward involvement, in order to return with renewed vigor to meet life's challenges.'" Everything around you can inspire or teach you, if you animate your gaze with a questing mind.

23

Live as much as possible at the center between all opposites. Everything is dual; that is how the one Spirit manifested its Creation. Every up is balanced by a down; light is always balanced by darkness; pleasure, by pain; emotional love, by hatred. (I say "emotional love," because there is no opposite to divine love; nor is there a balancing opposite to divine joy.) Eternal truths lie at the center, between all opposites. Therefore I say, live more at your center, in the heart, and in the heart chakra of your spine.

24

Whenever you feel pain or sorrow, withdraw from that feeling and become centered in yourself. Watch the pain from that center. Tell yourself, "This pain is not I; it is happening only to my body and ego. I am not those dream images."

25

One way to handle pain and sorrow is to visualize your consciousness expanded in space. If, for instance, you are sitting in a dentist's chair, tell yourself, "What happens to this body is occurring at only a tiny point in the vast reality around me."

26

A way to handle pain and sorrow is to expand your consciousness backward and forward in time. Tell yourself, "What is happening now is only flotsam on the river of time." Dwell on the thought of the Eternal Bliss you will know when you attain inner freedom. The ability to rise above the present moment is vital to that achievement.

27

An excellent way to rise above physical pain is to concentrate one-pointedly on something else. For example, when sitting in the dentist's chair (I haven't taken Novocain in years), I've composed music, or mentally worked out some passage in a book I was writing. I've found, with this practice, that whatever the dentist did to me was hardly worth noticing (though he, as many dentists have told me later, was sweating in sympathetic pain!).

28

Offer up every suffering to God. People speak with kindred pain of Christ's suffering on the cross. In truth he was *happy* to offer himself up in sacrifice for others. He took their karma onto his own body. But he himself was far above human pain. He had, in fact, no ego with which to suffer it, though he identified with it temporarily for the sake of suffering humanity! Inwardly, however, he knew only joy. What saddened him was man's indifference to God.

29

Face every trial cheerfully. Don't shrink from it, but thrust your chest out, and accept your tests bravely. Remember, you cannot avoid trouble anyway. Trials are like dogs: When they threaten you, confront them courageously; they'll lose heart, then, and flee. But if you run from them, they will give eager chase.

30

No calamity will be able to shake you, if you stand calmly at your own inner center. Form clearly in your mind the image my Guru gave in saying, "Be able to stand unshaken amidst the crash of breaking worlds!" Even in a cataclysm, if your heart remains firmly committed to God, terror will pass you by like a dark cloud, and you will find yourself enclosed in His bliss.

31

Seek the approval of people whose opinions you respect. The applause of multitudes is like rising bubbles in a glass of champagne, bursting at the surface. Better the scolding of wise men than the adulation of fools. A vote of popularity is the surest indication of mediocrity.

September

September

1

Whatever you do or accomplish, approach it with enthusiasm. Once you've finished it, however, release the project into the infinite. Don't keep dwelling on what you've accomplished so far, for in that case you'll find yourself unable to concentrate on new accomplishments. I sometimes find it difficult to remember the names of songs I have written, though I love them. They're done, now; they're in the past, and I've new images to mold. When my parents died, I used the inheritance they left me to create a home and garden for myself, and also for the Ananda community. The garden is as lovely as any I've seen anywhere. My father never gave a penny to my work, so I didn't want him to suffer in the other world by seeing me give his money to Ananda. My solution was to create a home of great beauty, surrounded by exceptionally lovely gardens, and to offer this place to our whole community for its spiritual center. At present, I live far away in Pune, India, within a noisy and dusty construction site. I am perfectly happy. Somehow, from a perennial zero one can accomplish so much more than when his zero is preceded by many numerals.

2

Give credit to others for anything you accomplish together. Indeed, give more credit to them than you accept for yourself. I remember my father commenting with a wry smile on the foreword written in French to a new book by a subordinate: "I recommend this book, which was written at my direction and under my constant supervision." What had that old fogey gained, except a few chuckles of derision? If a team helps you, presumably it is because you need them. And if you do need them, honor them by giving them as much of the credit as possible.

3

Look at, or imagine, a river, flowing constantly. Then visualize your thoughts flowing with similar steadfastness—not hopping about restlessly like frogs; nor drifting sluggishly, as if burdened with sludge; nor frozen motionless, like sheets of ice, with little floes of fixed ideas and opinions. Adapt yourself to circumstances. The more centered you are within, the easier you'll find it to change as the need arises. Affirm silently: "I adapt like flowing water to every new situation and idea."

4

Think of all the setbacks, failures, and disappointments you've had in life. Toss them up mentally into the air, like flower petals. Watch them float away with the wind, diminishing in size with distance, until they disappear. Finally, affirm joyously, "In my heart, I am free!"

5

Devote less time to being passively entertained—for instance, by watching television, or listening to music. Commit yourself to doing things, yourself. Don't work from your ego center, but offer yourself up as a clear channel for the Divine Creator. Passivity is to creativity what aimless floating is to swimming. And channeling God's grace is to egoic creativity what swimming with the current is to the struggle of swimming against it.

6

Be thoughtful, not absent-minded, when communicating with others. Absent-mindedness induces vague thinking, which in turn leads to chronic failure. If you mean what you say, and say it with focused attention, you will develop the power to succeed at anything you attempt.

September

7

Speak from a center of inner silence. Too much chatter is anesthetizing. A man in Calcutta once asked a young man, "My boy, are you married?" "What do you mean, Am I married? I'm married to your own daughter!" "Oh, I know, I know. I just wanted something to say, and could think of nothing else." Wouldn't the older man have done better, in this case, simply to remain silent? When you speak from the heart of silence, everything you say will have meaning.

8

Make a special effort today to break out of some mental self-enclosure—whether of selfishness, or timidity, or self-preoccupation. The quest for true maturity is entirely a matter of breaking out of one's high-walled mental prison. Expand your awareness to include the needs of other people. Then expand it further by sympathizing with those needs. Enlarge it still further, by helping them to fulfill their needs. Next, release whatever hold your own needs exert over you. Tell yourself, finally, "It is not I who am helping anyone: I only serve as a channel for God's grace." The feeling will come to you at last: "He alone is acting through me; He alone is the Doer."

9

Remain always, as my Guru put it, "even-minded and cheerful." Watch a cork bobbing on the waves of a lake: up and down, up and down, never straying off in any other direction; almost all its movement is up and down in the same place. Don't bob similarly on waves of emotion. You'll never get anywhere so long as you spend your time reacting to external events in your life. Be an *initiator*. Move serenely through life's waters, ever centered in your own spine.

10

View your problems dispassionately, as if from a mountain peak. Perspective is lost in the narrow valleys of personal involvement. But life's problems are tiny compared to your entire reality. If you allow them to loom large before you, they may overwhelm you. Yet in fact they are only small specks on a vast panorama.

11

See yourself, when you help others, as though you were a gardener watering plants. Whether the plants be bushes, grasses, or flowers, all of them need water. And all men need nourishment, whether they be haughty or humble, harsh or gentle, ignorant or learned, provocative or submissive, dry and brittle or richly humorous. And all of them will thrive, when nourished by the water of kindness.

12

Truth cannot be learned: it must be recognized. If you want to assist others to know the truth, state your thoughts simply; get others to respect your thoughts rather than you, for having uttered them. State those thoughts in such a way as to bring them back to people's remembrance. The sage Patanjali defined enlightenment itself as *smriti*: memory.

13

Be modest—even self-effacing. But don't belittle your-self. Self-deprecation, too, demands a focus on the ego. There should be neither superiority nor inferiority com-plex. Concentrate on the *what* of things, not on the *who*.

14

Never complain, no matter what you have to endure. Misfortune lies always in the perception of things, not in the things themselves. Should you suddenly lose all your wealth (perhaps in a stock market crash), in God's plan the time may have come for you to taste poverty. A positive lesson you can learn from the sudden loss is calm detachment. Another lesson is to be complete in yourself. Success and failure, both, are part of life's flow. So also are wealth and poverty, fame and ignominy, and gain and loss of every kind. Accept all opposites with a smile, for in God alone is it possible to rise above duality permanently. Meanwhile, accept your lot in life, what-ever it be, with good cheer. Remember, it's all a show—a cosmic dream. To your deeper Self, it has no reality.

September

15

In life's race, compete only against yourself. Sooner or later in this world of relativities, however skilled you may be, there will always be someone better. Every record is eventually broken. In the battle between good and evil, win against yourself. Be calmer today than you have ever been. Be kinder, more forgiving, more accepting, less judgmental. Whatever your faults and virtues, give more and more energy to the side of virtue.

16

Concentrate on the details of what you do; at the same time, exert willpower to refer those details constantly to your ultimate purpose. To keep them attuned to their true purpose is one of the secrets of genius—a point on which I disagree with dictionary definitions of this word. True genius comes from the superconscious; it is inspired by God. Whatever you do, offer your efforts up constantly to Him, for higher guidance.

17

When troubles beset you, seek both cause and solution at their true source: yourself. Karmic law rules supreme in the universe. Your every act in the past represented a movement away from your unmoving center, the inner Self. That movement will forever demand the compensation of an equal, opposite movement. Though hindered by what my Guru called "the thwarting cross-currents of ego," the law must, sooner or later, be fulfilled. These back-and-forth movements never proceed in straight lines. Rather, they create eddies which draw into their vortex the debris of countless desires and involvements. Don't trouble yourself with the complexity of life, but seek ever the divine simplicity of oneness with God's joy. To do otherwise is to court further, unending troubles.

18

How shall you define God? Think of Him (or Her) as the highest potential you can imagine for yourself. God is that, and much more. As the Bhagavad Gita* states, He is, in all things, their supremest manifestation: Supreme Power, Wisdom, Love, Joy, Peace, Fulfillment, Satisfaction, Beauty, and Contentment.

---

* India's favorite scripture.

19

You have within yourself the power to overcome all adversity. Even should you be made a slave, or thrown into a dungeon without hope of release, no one can enslave your mind. If you cannot conquer a difficulty outwardly, you can still rise above it inwardly. Seek freedom in yourself. That freedom can be denied you by no one. Were utter failure to crash down, wavelike, upon you, know that God's law is ever just and benign. Place yourself in His hands, and everything *must* turn out, eventually, for the best.

20

There is only one key to happiness: it lies within yourself. Earthly happiness is like a rainbow, radiant in its many colors, but evanescent, and formed of mere mist: the raindrops of earthly sorrow! When you can welcome the rain as gladly as the rainbow—the one bringing cleansing to the heart, the other bringing delight—you can be happy always.

September

21

Challenges were sent to stimulate you, and to help you in your spiritual growth. Twice, when I was a child, bullies much larger and stronger than I attacked me and gave me a thorough beating. Both times I won against them in time, mentally, by never admitting defeat. From then on they gave me a wide berth. Never surrender mentally to anyone. People before whom you maintain your own integrity may go so far as to call you a traitor. Let them say what they will: you remain strong in yourself. If your will can be preserved unbroken, you will always come out on top in the end.

22

If any mood oppresses you, offer it into a wider perception of reality. Moods are like waves, which, no matter how high they rise, never change the ocean level. Live at that point of equilibrium in yourself, where nothing can affect you.

September

23

All equality is a delusion, except in the oneness of God. Otherwise, life is like a ladder. The animals are helped up that ladder by association—usually as pets—with human beings. Less aware and less creative people are helped upward by serving in the homes of people who are more highly evolved. Originally, the caste system in India wasn't hereditary, and wasn't meant to suppress anybody, but was intended to indicate the ideal direction of human development: from body-bound (*kayastha*) to freedom from ego. "One moment in the company of a saint," it is said, "will be your raft over the ocean of delusion." The company of saints is vitally important for those who want God, and most important of all is attunement with, and inner surrender to, one's own guru.

24

Don't be a climber outwardly, whether socially or in any other way. Even in the ashrams of saints I have seen people play that game. Absorb whatever virtues attract you in others, but never try to impress anybody. Move through social groups like a ship sailing serenely through heavy waters. Be complete in yourself, until you see some quality you'd like to take on as a "passenger." Divine illumination will carry you finally beyond all human, egoic qualities. Seek those qualities, therefore, which will help you to reach inner freedom.

25

Learn to cooperate with others, even if their interests differ from your own. Never surrender your principles, however, no matter what the consequence to your popularity. The guiding principle in your life should not be egoic self-interest, but God's will. Even if you should be burned at the stake for adhering to the truth as you know it: Truth alone free you from all suffering forever.

26

What makes a man noble is not land, money, or social standing, but character. Be true to your word; generous in action; forgiving of every wrong; courteous to all (even to the lowest beggar); and always deferential to the truth. A true nobleman is one whose character is always firmly upright.

27

Pay little heed to people's opinions, including your own. Truth is not a matter of opinion. Truth simply *is*.

28

True politeness is not a mask. It is born of the soul's innate dignity, which helps one to see in everybody, everywhere, the one presence of God. Respect all, as brothers and sisters in the one family of our common Father.

29

Good manners are innate. They are born of respect, dignity, kindness, and good will. Customs vary from country to country, and from place to place within each country. For those who travel much, it is impossible to keep up with all those conventions. Much more important than such trivia as table manners are attitudes that ennoble the human spirit.

30

If people treat you haughtily or condescendingly, don't react. Be polite but distant in your behavior toward them. Let them see that, whatever opinion they hold of you, they have your respect and good will, but not your deference. Never court anyone's good opinion, but hear people's opinions impersonally. Defer to wisdom, but never to ignorance.

October

1

"Fame and wealth," my Guru used to say, "are like prostitutes: loyal to no man." In the end, these two bring only disappointment. If fame comes unasked, however, owing to some past karma (I hesitate to call it *good* karma!), use it for the benefit of others, and not to bolster your own ego. Fame can be a means of reaching many people, and helping them; never glory in it, however. You are the same person, whether known or unknown. It is easier to be yourself, however, if people don't burden you with their expectations. Be natural with them, open—even deferential—to their opinions.

October

2

Wealth, if it comes to you, should be treated as a sacred trust. It is not yours, even if you've worked hard to earn it. Karma (again, it will be *good* karma only if you use it rightly) has put you in this position so that you may help others. Use it to make this a better world to live in. Otherwise, wealth can suffocate one's finer feelings. Try occasionally to live in voluntary poverty. Many years ago, I lived for three months on ten dollars a month; what others might have seen as deprivation was, to me, a worthwhile challenge. It is amazing how happily one can live on almost nothing. Live simply. One delusion of wealth is that it tends to make a person feel himself superior to others. It also makes one self-protective against favor-seekers. When you travel, try if possible to go incognito. Treat all as your equals; remember, though poor financially, they may be rich in ways that preclude the possession of money. *Appreciate* them for what they are.

3

If you are poor, remember, your karma *can* be improved. Poverty means that the normal flow of divine abundance has, in your case, been somehow blocked — whether by past avarice, or selfishness, or indifference to others' needs, or by scattering your forces heedlessly. You can remove that block by offering your energy into the divine flow. A strong bad karma cannot, of course, be completely nullified, but its effects can be mitigated. The more you allow God to flow through you, the more everything in your life will improve.

4

Non-attachment is true wealth. If one is attached, he is always afraid of loss. And if he fears to lose anything, he has in a sense lost it already. Attachment is an attitude that many carry to the end of life. An old man, lying on his deathbed, cried out to his son, "Trim that lamp wick, son! The oil is being wasted." His own life was already all-but consumed, and still he worried about saving money! A person who is non-attached wants nothing. And nothing is all that one needs to possess, if he is rich in God.

October

5

Learn when to stop whatever you are doing. If speaking, learn to stop when you've said enough. If writing, don't drag on past the point you are making. In both cases, people often think, "If I can say just a little more, I'll convince a few more people." After driving your listeners to the top of a cliff, however, all you can do, further, is push them over the edge. Stop also when you feel you've *done* enough. After writing a little over 400 pieces of music, I felt I'd said what I'd wanted to say in that medium. That was over ten years ago, and since then I've not written a note. If ever I decide I have more to say, I'll say it; otherwise, it's better to remain silent. After taking some 15,000 photographs, I decided that was enough. For some time I took my camera with me to beautiful places, including the famous Engadine valley in Switzerland, but throughout my week there I never once took the camera out of my suitcase.

6

Not a thought that you can think originates with you. Paramhansa Yogananda, in *Autobiography of a Yogi*, wrote, "Thoughts are universally and not individually rooted." No thought is your own: It catches currents of consciousness that flow through the universe. The universe we live in is a manifestation of consciousness. Therefore Yogananda said also, "I suffer when you have moods, for I see then that Satan has got ahold of you." Think, when a negative outlook wells up within you, "A negative influence is clutching at me." To rid yourself of any chance of such "possession," chant to God, and raise your level of consciousness in the spine. Soon, more positive thoughts and feelings will start to appear in your mind.

7

Emanate peaceful thoughts; they'll create a shining aura of peace all around you, forming a protective barrier. The agitation in your world will no longer be able to touch you.

October

8

Don't worry about others' opinions; don't even pay attention to what they say or think about you—unless you think that, by listening, you might learn something worthwhile. Think of others in terms of what you give out to them, not of what you receive in return.

9

Love people, if not for themselves (many human traits, after all, are not in themselves lovable!), then for the pure joy of loving all.

10

If you feel impelled to defend a principle, never do so under the influence of anger. Defend the principle joyously! *Dharmic* (righteous) causes should be defended dharmically, and joyous non-attachment is a very high dharma.

October

11

Wrap yourself in a cloak of inner calmness. A strong, calm will, wisely guided, will be your best protection against all adversity.

12

Never defend your mistakes. People who do so are only defending their egos. The more readily you admit an error, the easier it will be to change yourself, and win final release from ego-consciousness. Be always sure, then, to take the next step: *Do* try to change! Years ago, when playing volleyball, I cheerfully claimed every error our side made. I remember someone on the other team finally crying out, "Your humility is inspiring, *but when will you reform?!*"

October

13

Rid yourself of all self-definitions. They will limit *you*, the ever-perfect soul. As an individual, you are unique, for God never makes even two snowflakes exactly alike. Self-definitions are like baggage that people lug around: the heavier the bags, the slower the movement. The more you renounce your self-definitions, the easier it will be for you to change in all ways, and change quickly, for you'll have less and less to carry, and be increasingly free in yourself.

14

"**P**eople are more important than things." This is a basic principle at our Ananda communities, which my Guru founded through me. It is a good principle to practice in your life, also: not things, only, but plans and projects of all kinds. Consideration for people will help to ground your ideas. It will also help to ensure that what you do is right.

15

Even though you are non-attached, hold cheerful expectations of life. Whatever comes, meet it with a smile; your cheerfulness will magnetically draw to you the best results.

16

Reach out with sympathy to others; don't wait for them to reach out first to you. There are many stricken and wounded on life's battlefield. People try to protect their hurt feelings, for fear of being smitten again. Thus, they will sometimes act toward you with seeming coldness. Be a spiritual medic. Go out of your way to help them, especially those who are in psychological pain, or in spiritual doubt. It's amazing what a warm smile can do to melt the blocks of ice which enclose so many hearts.

17

Face trials, obstacles, and opposition courageously. You are a child of God, and as such are the equal of anyone on earth. You have the infinite potential to achieve greatness—indeed, perfection. A painting should be judged in its finished state, not by mistakes the artist makes while his work is still in progress.

18

Give others their due—and, indeed, more than their due, to make sure you're not giving it grudgingly. In that spirit of generosity, allow others also to give you your due, though reminding them, "God is the Doer." To reject sincere praise in the name of humility is to impugn the judgment and good taste of those who offer it.

19

Be humble, but never abject. True humility is not self-abasement, but the contemplation of, and later the complete absorption in, broader realities. In bright sunlight, the light of a candle is so dimmed it may shine unnoticed.

20

Stand courageously by whatever lessons you've learned in life. Others may urge you to think differently, but the only truths you can ever know are those which you've experienced yourself. Change your thinking only when new experiences oblige you to see things differently.

21

To be dignified is not necessarily to be proud, pompous, or conceited. It can also mean that you live calmly at your own center. A person of true dignity recognizes, and bows to, the divine in all others. He is open to their views and suggestions, but weighs them always against his own understanding, born of experience.

22

Never allow yourself, out of hurt feelings, to shut your heart's door against others. Locking that door brings its own pain. You can no more control how others treat you than you can control the weather. Your behavior toward them, however, and how you treat them, is under your control. Rather than let a hurt seal your heart, ask yourself, "Is there any sense in suffering twice?"

October

23

Concentrate your powers, if you want to succeed in life. To penetrate a field of ice, don't press down on the whole lake: press at one spot with a sharp instrument. With calm, concentrated force, you can bring to success even the most impossible-seeming undertakings.

24

Wish everybody the best, and life will always work with you. Bless everybody, and you yourself will be blessed. You will receive from the world exactly what you put out to it, and to the same degree.

25

Never be afraid to give love, even if your feelings are unrequited or disdained. True love wants nothing in return. It does not hold out a begging bowl to others. It enriches the giver, for one is always affected by whatever feelings one channels to others. On the other hand, if you withhold love, you yourself will become dead, inside. Feelings are like flowing water: when prevented from movement, they stagnate.

26

Dare to dream greatness. But don't seek it in the world's eyes. Worldly approval is like a house built on sand. Seek approval in the eyes of the Unbribable Judge, God, and of His saints, His angels, and those who live by truth. To dream greatness is not a presumption if it means dreaming of performing good deeds. Dream of doing something worthwhile for others. Above all, try to fulfill God's will for you in your life, and ask Him to help you as you strive to help all.

27

Think of yourself as a student of truth and of life, and not as anyone's teacher. If you find yourself in a teaching role, feel what a privilege it is to share with others what you yourself have learned in life. Above all, never let yourself feel that people owe it to you to accept anything you teach.

October

28

If anything in other people displeases you, think, "What does it matter? There will always be something wrong in this world. Perhaps the only thing I can do about it is rid myself of my own displeasure." What displeases us about others, often, is something we have to overcome in ourselves. Learn to accept things as they are. Change them if you can, without anger or disdain, but realize that there is too much wrong in the world for you really to improve it very much. Your own essential need will be simply to learn how not to be affected, personally.

29

Has something or someone angered you? If so, work to correct that corrosive emotion in yourself. Reflect: someday—perhaps even tomorrow—you'll have moved on to other concerns. Why stew in anger today? It is you, yourself, who are being cooked! Do nothing about the situation until you've regained your equilibrium.

30

If you are angry, it may be because your idea of how things ought to be has been outraged. Reflect on how very many views are held on virtually every subject. Find the rest point within yourself, midway between all opposites. Dwell there calmly. Only when you are calm inside can you address every issue with true insight.

31

If you become angry, drink these antidotes: kindness, concern for others, and good will. Be like Jesus who, during a storm, commanded the waves, "Peace. Be still." Anger, like a disease, can upset the whole body: the digestion; the nervous system; the heart rate; the breath; even one's mental clarity. Is it really worth all that trouble over something you'll be unlikely to change anyway?

November

November

1

Egotism is different from egoism. A friend of mine in college once asked me the difference, and almost without thinking I replied, "Egotism is pride. Egoism is excessive consciousness of self." I still consider this the best definition of the difference between these two words. Both words describe qualities that must be overcome, but of the two, egoism is much the subtler. The best way out of it is to *give* of oneself—to others; to what you believe in; to God.

2

Consideration for others is a sign of maturity. It shows sensitivity to others and to their needs. All this is part of man's struggle out of the quicksands of egoism.

3

Never accuse or confront anyone. First ask him, as supportively as possible, "Did you do it?" And then ask, "Why?" Give him the benefit of any doubt. If no doubt exists, at least respect his right to make his own mistakes. In this way, he will know that you are his friend. And isn't that a consideration you yourself would like from everybody?

4

Dress not for admiration, but to give pleasure to others. Often I have thanked even perfect strangers, both male and female, for wearing something colorful or pleasing to the eye. Color especially, if well chosen, can make everyone's day a little brighter. In thanking people, however, try not to convey an impression that you have any ulterior motive.

5

Make everything you do an act of outward giving from yourself. In this way you will combat natural egoism, by expanding your reality beyond the boundaries of self-involvement to include all life.

6

Never accept anything on the strength of its popularity. Don't worry if it makes you seem quaint in others' eyes. Be true to yourself, to your own tastes, your own views of right and wrong. One road leads to truth; the other, into the dense fogs of delusion.

7

In judging good taste, whether in music or in the other arts, ask yourself, "What does this piece do to my consciousness? Does it soothe me? Is it an influence for harmony, wisdom, or some other wholesome quality?" To produce good art requires much more than skill, for the arts represent states of consciousness. Ask yourself, "Would I like to receive someone in my home who exudes this state of consciousness?"

8

One's taste in food can be an indication of, and can also influence, one's state of consciousness. Eat only food that is rich in life and energy; don't eat stale or "dead" food. Fresh food will serve you best. Don't eat food if it is excessively stimulating, nor food that is excessively bland. Foods contain different vibrations. For this reason it is good to abstain from eating meat, especially that of animals which are conscious enough to feel fear and anger at being slaughtered. People who eat such meat (as distinct from fish, fowl, and lamb) absorb into themselves similar vibrations. In eating, concentrate on taste, rather than bolting your food down absent-mindedly. The more you enjoy your food—not gluttonously, but with calm appreciation—the more you will absorb its wholesome vibrations.

9

When others speak idly or foolishly, don't let yourself be drawn into their orbit of consciousness. Be respectful, but remain, as much as possible, reserved and silent. Idle chatter, like radio static, prevents one from penetrating to the truth of things.

November

10

Don't try to be stylish. People who follow the current styles reveal, in their attempt to be *de la mode*, their own lack of taste. The modern styles presented in newspapers and magazines are often shocking, garish, and bizarre. Their message is: "Look! Look at me!" Their whole purpose is to get people to look, and to keep on looking, even if it be in horror or dismay. To be tasteful is always to be understated. Indeed, to me, understatement is the very essence of good taste.

11

Keep a sense of humor, especially when things don't turn out as you hoped. Life is a play: often, a tragicomedy. To enjoy the play, be disinvolved enough in it to realize that the scenes will keep changing, and that, even if the play ends in tragedy, its effect may purify your feelings and expand your consciousness.

November

12

Don't bludgeon others with your sense of humor, if you find them unreceptive to it. Having offered a thought in fun, remain good-humored and kind, but respect them in their lack of receptivity.

13

Before making any important decision in life, consult, in inner silence, your higher Self. You can ask inwardly for the right answer and receive it in a second, if you direct your question toward the spiritual eye in the forehead, asking, "Is this the right decision? If not, what should I do?" If then you consult your heart, the answer will appear, as if "ready made." It depends on how strongly you direct your energy while asking the question. Others may take months to reach a conclusion, and will often reach a wrong one anyway, because they look for it only to be *reasonable*.

14

Be graceful in your movements. Awkward or jerky gestures reflect, and also induce, disconnected thinking. Graceful movements, on the other hand, will help bring a smooth flow to your thoughts.

15

Have the courage to embrace the unexpected. Life is an ever-unfolding drama. If you embrace affirmatively whatever happens—and don't merely accept it—you will find that you can turn even difficult circumstances to good advantage.

16

Inspire others by example more than by words. And inspire them more by your vibrations than by the example you set. An act of goodness, for example, may or may not be understood in the spirit it was meant, but a *vibration* of goodness will radiate its influence even at a distance. In the last analysis, inspiration goes far *beyond* mere analysis! It is a vibration of conscious feeling.

17

Think before you speak. Be circumspect in both speech and action. Don't, by unseemly haste or carelessness, expose yourself to misunderstanding, and never embroil yourself in controversy unnecessarily.

18

Receive praise good-humoredly. Reflect that the compliments you receive today may be withdrawn tomorrow, and that even deserved praise carries with it the danger of adding to your burden of self-definitions which, in the quest for happiness, you should try resolutely to eliminate.

19

Give praise sincerely but understatedly. Never flatter anyone. Praise should, in other words, be addressed to the God in others, not to their egos, for you should always try, as their friend, to assist them in their efforts to scale the spiritual heights.

November

20

Don't compare yourself with others, either to your advantage or to their detriment. On a freeway, there are as many cars ahead of as behind you. Once you've worked your way to the front of one cluster, you'll only find yourself last in the next cluster. Simply go your way, thinking only of reaching your own destination.

21

Your magnetic effect on others depends on your state of consciousness. That effect cannot but exist, but never exert it on anyone hypnotically. Let your influence be an aura of light that you carry with you wherever you go. Try to affect others beneficially; leave it to them, however, to accept as much from you, or as little, as they choose.

22

Emanate peace in all directions around you. Harmonize the vibrations in your heart, then consciously expand those vibrations into your environment, and into the hearts of all whom you contact.

November

23

Beware of the influence of feeling on reason. To suppress your feelings would be merely to distort their influence on your mind. Refine your feelings, rather, to the pure gold of intuition. Thus, you will always, and in everything you do, be guided rightly.

24

Move through life as though you were on a ski run. Don't treat it as a game of chess, in which every move is carefully plotted in advance. Bring a flow in your life. That flow can be disturbed by too-careful reasoning. Rely more on the guidance of calm intuition.

25

Treat others as colleagues, not as competitors, even when all of you work at the same activity. A thousand streams, when they meet, flow together to become a mighty river. Thus, indeed, are great civilizations born.

26

Listen always for the voice of good counsel. If you hold yourself truly open, you may hear it even in the wind.

27

Seek wisdom from experience more than from books. When you encounter teachings in a book, ask yourself always, "Does this resonate with my own experience?" If it doesn't, don't scoff at it, for it may be a truth you simply have yet to discover. And don't accept it, either; simply put it on "hold." You can really know a truth only when you've actually lived it.

28

Above all, be loyal to the truth as you understand it. And tell the truth, no matter how inconvenient for you. Though your friends and relatives try to influence you otherwise, be faithful to the truth as you yourself have experienced it.

November

29

Make originality a philosophy of life—not in the sense of trying to be different, for true originality means to proceed from one's point of origin, in himself. It doesn't mean doing something no one has ever done before. Rather, it means developing your own perceptions. Those same thoughts may have occurred to millions of other people. Never borrow, or react to, the thoughts and actions of others. A thought will be original if it comes from your own perceptions of life.

30

Seek, in recreation, to re-create yourself. During every pause between activities, seek, through inner peace and relaxation, a renewal of the creative spirit. Withdraw into your inner temple of silence, there to focus and re-energize your thoughts.

December

December

1

Expect success, but don't let that expectation take the place of painstaking effort. People who brag about what they will accomplish all too often overlook the little steppingstones of detail over which one treads his way to success.

2

Do nothing for applause. Act for the far more satisfying approval of your own conscience. Someone once asked me, "What has motivated you to do all the things you've done?" Conscience? yes, certainly. But conscience, in my case, in reaction to the great suffering I see in the world, born of people's ignorance as to who and what they really are: children of God.

3

Do your best, then leave the consequences to themselves. Attachment to the results only diminishes one's ability to work effectively in the present. But with non-attachment, even if you fail in one endeavor, you will be free to direct your energy anew, and ever yet anew, until success is achieved.

December

4

Practice patience. Patience is the straight, smooth highway to success. Patience will keep you inwardly calm, not overreactive to difficulties, and always able to adjust to, and handle sensibly, any difficulty you encounter.

5

Show respect for convention, but remember that many conventions were started by unconventional, or at least independent-minded, people. Why do people stand when their national anthem is being played? It must have begun with one person; no one wanted to show disrespect, so everyone followed his example. Why do people stand for the "Hallelujah" chorus in Handel's *Messiah*? Because King George of England did so first; everyone else had to stand because he did. Most conventions have no intrinsic meaning. Usually, it would make only a foolish statement to rebel against them; they help to hold society together. Follow convention to be sociable, but *respect* it only if your reason confirms its validity. Ignore conventions, however, if they are harmful or demeaning to others.

December

6

Some conventions, certainly, must be changed. Racial discrimination in America, for example, is an abomination—a means of suppression, a cause of bigotry, and a fetter to the ego in all who practice it. So also is the caste system in India, which in its origins was enlightened—when it was not hereditary, but pointed the way to salvation. When the caste system was made hereditary, however, the same misfortunes appeared as happened with racial discrimination in America. See all human beings as your own brothers and sisters: equals before God.

7

Don't ask yourself, "How can I do this differently?" Don't even ask, "How can I do it better?" until you've asked first, "What is the right thing to do, and the *right* way to go about doing it?"

December

8

Let others, if they will, see you as their enemy. Resolve, for your part, to be their friend. More than one person has said to me, "I don't know why I hate you." I know why: I am true to myself, not to their desires and expectations of me. But I always answer, "I know only that I am your friend, and will always wish you well."

9

To attract abundance, see money as a flow of energy, not as a static quantity. See life itself also as a flow, not as a fixed pattern. A drinking glass can hold only so much liquid; even so, your little brain can hold only so many thoughts. Leave your ego on the bank, and enter the flowing river of cosmic awareness. There is no limit to how much of life's abundance—not only money, but wealth of all kinds—can be yours, if you will offer yourself into that eternal flow.

10

If you want to improve your circumstances, work first on improving yourself. To desire better treatment from others is to enslave yourself to them. Become in everything a cause, not an effect. Self-dependence is independence, and the mark of true heroism.

11

Include the success of others in your quest for personal success. Better a stream that makes the whole valley green than an oasis, surrounded by vast stretches of sand.

12

Attachment, like an unripe fruit, clings to its branch even when buffeted by high winds. Be, instead, like a ripened fruit, which releases its hold instantly when touched by the lightest breeze of threatened suffering.

December

13

A true friend is one you can weep with, not only one with whom you can laugh. Be such a friend to others. Let them feel your care for them in their sorrows. Weep with them, sometimes—not in such a way as to increase their woes, but only to wean them from it. Never weep, however, for yourself.

14

Think vastness! Think eternity! Don't limit yourself to present realities, whether in space or in time. Your very thoughts are but waves on the vast ocean of consciousness.

15

Love others as aspects of your own Self. Every individual specializes on behalf of the whole race in being himself. Each is evolving a specific expression of potentials that are universal to all.

December

16

If someone ridicules you, laugh with him if you can. Otherwise, if he is guilty of mere buffoonery, look away in calm silence. But if he mocks your principles, answer him as he deserves: "Mockery comes easily, to the ignorant." Has someone slighted you? Thank him. Has someone hurt your feelings? Thank him. Has someone tried to destroy your work, or your reputation? In all such opposition, give thanks. Certainly you should try at least to protect whatever worthwhile work you are doing; you may even have to fight for it. Your thanks, however, will be for the reminders your enemies give you that all is *maya*: delusion. True satisfaction will come to you only when you've escaped its clutches forever.

17

As you wash your body, so also, at the end of each day, cleanse your heart of every impurity of desire and attachment, and of every wrong thought you have held, or wrong words you have expressed, to anyone.

December

18

Imagine every difficulty, every desire, every attachment soaring up like a balloon, shrinking with distance until it disappears altogether. Then return to your essential Self: enjoy your release into inner freedom.

19

The Italians have a saying, "If it isn't true, at least it's well said (*se non è vero, è ben trovato*)." Don't be lured too deeply by the attractive power of epigrams. Where truth is concerned, laugh if you like, but in the end, be serious.

December

20

Use discrimination in filtering the invasion of modern gadgetry into your life. If you embrace clever inventions too enthusiastically, you may sacrifice your inner freedom and peace of mind. Too much "gadget-addiction" can absorb energy unnecessarily, and for that reason is a qualified blessing. Granted, many such inventions are helpful, but if I myself want some piece of arcane information which might call for more research than I care to devote to getting it, I "farm" the job out to some friend who enjoys that kind of thing. In this way, I find I never need to explore the all-too-absorbing intricacies of "surfing" the internet. I prefer, in this case, to live in blissful ignorance. Even granting the great benefits the internet offers, the trouble with it is that it can burden the mind with trivia.

December

21

How **modern do we** owe it to our present age to be? I myself was born in the then-backward, nearly medieval land of Romania. Never have I made a strong effort to bring myself into the present age. Many scientific discoveries have swirled around me; new fads have sprung up; new slang; new ways of looking at things. I have chosen to remain untouched by any of it; to use it only as much as will help me (these pages, for instance, are being written on a computer); to pass serenely through the fairground of fresh excitements, but to let nothing reach me that might take me out of myself. I never watch television programs, unless for some very specific purpose. I don't care to be either modern or old-fashioned. Time passes, but divine truth remains forever unchanged.

Do It *Well!*

December

22

Never depend on your own powers alone. They are inevitably fragile, weak, and inconsistent. If you trust in God, however, you will find that, by asking Him for help, He will do everything you ask of Him provided you ask with faith. Don't plead with Him. Say, rather, "This is what I am trying to accomplish for You. I need Your strength, and Your guidance. I'll do what I can, but You must do the rest." Don't be afraid that He may think you presumptuous. He won't if you are humble, and if your desire is only to please Him. Many a job I've done successfully only after I'd said to God, "I can't do this, but *You* can do anything! So come along: Help me!"

23

Give up the thought, "This is mine! all mine!" Tell God, with regard to everything in your life, "This is Thine! all Thine! Nothing is my own except under franchise from Thee." The less you think of anything as your own, the freer you'll be in yourself. And the more you think of everything as His, the more joy will infuse your heart, until you find that *you*, yourself, are pure Bliss.

December

24

To be creative, first relax your mind. Every worthwhile task was originally conceived in the Infinite Mind.

25

The teachings of Jesus Christ, and of every great spiritual master, are as fresh and true today as they were when they were first uttered. Truth never changes with the times, though it may need to be presented differently, to meet changes in human understanding. Love, wisdom, joy, and every high virtue taught by those masters; above all their essential insights into eternal truth: none of these will ever change. There is no need to be a pulpit-pounding preacher. All that is needed is to know that the truths taught in the scriptures are ever one and the same, everywhere. Our souls came from God, and our eternal duty, forever, is to merge into Him at last.

26

You belong to all nations. Only temporarily are you an American, Frenchman, Italian, Indian; a Christian, Jew, Hindu, Buddhist, or Moslem. You belong to all classes. Your social class is only briefly upper, middle, or lower. No human condition defines you, for you are the pure soul, descended from God. *He*, for all eternity, is your essential, never-changing reality.

27

Don't identify people with their personalities. Identify them with the goodness of their intentions, and the sincerity with which they seek the truth. Our personalities are only consequences of our countless actions and reactions over many past incarnations, but the innate goodness of our intentions, and our soul-sincerity, have their origins at greater depths, in the Self.

December

28

Pour conscious energy into everything you do. Remember, energy has its own intelligence, and responds to intelligent handling. It can make things happen for you for which you yourself could never have planned.

29

Develop a sense of community with others. No one stands alone in this world, though to some people it may seem that the opposite is true, for we come into this life alone, and leave it also alone. Yet we come into a welcoming family, and should so live our lives that many weep when we leave. Everything we do, including all our solitary-seeming comings and goings, depends also on others. Expand your sense of community to embrace an ever-larger number of human beings, until you see the whole world as your own, in God.

30

Work on simplifying your view of life. Seek always, beneath its many bewildering patterns, life's underlying and ever-simple unity. Complex thinking only creates complexity in life, in work, in relationships. To be divinely childlike means to reclaim your divine simplicity.

31

Respect excellence wherever you find it. True excellence may be the result of group endeavor, but in each case it requires individual commitment of energy and awareness. Excellence, like everything that is worthwhile, springs from *within* one's own self.

About the Author

"Swami Kriyananda is a man of wisdom and compassion in action, truly one of the leading lights in the spiritual world today."
—Lama Surya Das, Dzogchen Center, author of *Awakening The Buddha Within*

SWAMI KRIYANANDA

A prolific author, accomplished composer, playwright, and artist, and a world-renowned spiritual teacher, Swami Kriyananda refers to himself simply as "a humble disciple" of the great God-realized master, Paramhansa Yogananda. He met his guru at the age of twenty-two, and served him during the last four years of the Master's life. And he has done so continuously ever since.

Kriyananda was born in Rumania of American parents, and educated in Europe, England, and the United States. Philosophically and artistically inclined from youth, he soon came to question life's meaning, and society's values. During a period of intense inward reflection, he discovered Yogananda's *Autobiography of a Yogi*, and immediately traveled three thousand miles from New York to California to meet the Master, who accepted him as a monastic disciple. Yogananda appointed him as the head of the monastery, authorized him to teach in his name and to give initiation into Kriya Yoga, and entrusted him with the mission of writing, and developing what he called "world-brotherhood colonies."

About the Author

Recognized as "the father of the spiritual communities movement" in the United States, Swami Kriyananda founded Ananda World Brotherhood Village in the Sierra Nevada Foothills of northern California in 1968. It has served as a model for seven communities founded subsequently in the United States, Europe, and India.

In 2003 Swami Kriyananda, then in his seventy-eighth year, moved to India with a small international group of disciples to dedicate his remaining years to making his guru's teachings better known in that country. He has established Ananda's third publishing company, all of which publish his one hundred-plus literary works and spread the teachings of Kriya Yoga throughout the world. His vision for the upcoming years includes, in India, founding cooperative spiritual communities (there are two communities there now, one in Gurgaon and the other near Pune); a temple of all religions dedicated to Paramhansa Yogananda; a retreat center; a school system; a monastery; as well as a university-level Yoga Institute of Living Wisdom.

Further Explorations

If you are inspired by *Do It* Well*!* and would like to learn more about Paramhansa Yogananda and his teachings, or about Swami Kriyananda, Crystal Clarity Publishers offers many additional resources to assist you.

Autobiography of a Yogi
Paramhansa Yogananda

Autobiography of a Yogi is one of the best selling Eastern philosophy titles of all time, with millions of copies sold. It has been named one of the best and most influential books of the twentieth century. This highly prized reprinting of the original 1946 edition is the only one available free from textual changes made after Yogananda's death.

Yogananda was the first yoga master of India whose mission was to live and teach in the West. His account of his life experiences includes childhood revelations, stories of his visits to saints and masters in India, and long-secret teachings of Self-realization that he made available to Western readers.

In this updated edition are bonus materials, including a last chapter that Yogananda wrote in 1951, without posthumous changes. This new edition also includes the eulogy that Yogananda wrote for Gandhi, and a new foreword and afterword by Swami Kriyananda, one of Yogananda's close, direct disciples.

Praise for *Autobiography of a Yogi*

"In the original edition, published during Yogananda's life, one is more in contact with Yogananda himself. While Yogananda founded centers and organizations, his concern was more with guiding individuals to direct communion with Divinity rather than with

Further Explorations

promoting any one church as opposed to another. This spirit is easier to grasp in the original edition of this great spiritual and yogic classic." —David Frawley, Director, American Institute of Vedic Studies, author of *Yoga and Ayurveda*

ALSO AVAILABLE IN:
52-Card Deck and Booklet: with images from the book
Unabridged Audiobook (MP3 format)

Revelations of Christ
Proclaimed by Paramhansa Yogananda,
Presented by His Disciple, Swami Kriyananda

Over the past years, our faith has been severely shaken by experiences such as the breakdown of church authority, discoveries of ancient texts that supposedly contradict long-held beliefs, and the sometimes outlandish historical analyses of Scripture by academics. Together, these forces have helped create confusion and uncertainty about the true teachings and meanings of Christ's life. Now, more than ever, people are yearning for a clear-minded, convincing, yet uplifting understanding of the life and teachings of Jesus Christ.

This soul-stirring book, presenting the teachings of Christ from the experience and perspective of Paramhansa Yogananda, one of the greatest spiritual masters of the twentieth century, finally offers the fresh understanding of Christ's teachings for which the world has been waiting. This book presents us with an opportunity to understand the Scriptures in a more reliable way than any other: by learning from those saints who have communed directly, in deep ecstasy, with Christ and God.

Further Explorations

Praise for *Revelations of Christ*

"This is a great gift to humanity. It is a spiritual treasure to cherish and to pass on to children for generations. This remarkable and magnificent book brings us to the doorway of a deeper, richer embracing of Eternal Truth."—Neale Donald Walsch, author of Conversations with God

"Kriyananda's revelatory book gives us the enlightened, timeless wisdom of Jesus the Christ in a way that addresses the challenges of twenty-first century living."—Michael Beckwith, founder and Spiritual Director, Agape International Spiritual Center, author of *Inspirations of the Heart*

ALSO AVAILABLE IN:
Audiobook (MP3 format)

The Essence of the Bhagavad Gita
Explained by Paramhansa Yogananda
As Remembered by His Disciple,
Swami Kriyananda

Rarely in a lifetime does a new spiritual classic appear that has the power to change people's lives and transform future generations. This is such a book.

This revelation of India's best-loved scripture approaches it from a fresh perspective, showing its deep allegorical meaning and its down-to-earth practicality. The themes presented are universal: how to achieve victory in life in union with the divine; how to prepare for life's "final exam," death, and what happens afterward; how to triumph over all pain and suffering.

Praise for *The Essence of the Bhagavad Gita*

'The Essence of the Bhagavad Gita *is a brilliant text that will greatly enhance the spiritual life of every reader."*—Caroline Myss, author of *Anatomy of the Spirit* and *Sacred Contracts*

Further Explorations

Praise for The Essence of the Bhagavad Gita, *continued.*

"It is doubtful that there has been a more important spiritual writing in the last fifty years than this soul-stirring, monumental work. What a gift! What a treasure!" —Neale Donald Walsch, author of *Conversations with God*

ALSO AVAILABLE IN:
Audiobook (MP3 format)
Also available as paperback without commentary, titled
The Bhagavad Gita.

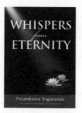

Whispers from Eternity
Paramhansa Yogananda
Edited by His Disciple, Swami Kriyananda

Many poetic works can inspire, but few, like this one, have the power to change your life. Yogananda was not only a spiritual master, but a master poet, whose poems revealed the hidden divine presence behind even everyday things.

Open this book, pick a poem at random, and read it. Mentally repeat whatever phrase appeals to you. Within a short time, you will feel your consciousness transformed. This book has the power to rapidly accelerate your spiritual growth, and provides hundreds of delightful ways for you to begin your own conversation with God.

ALSO AVAILABLE IN:
Audiobook (MP3 format)

Do It *Well!*

Further Explorations

The Wisdom of Yogananda Series

This series features writings of Paramhansa Yogananda not available elsewhere. These books include writings from his earliest years in America, in an approachable, easy-to-read format. The words of the Master are presented with minimal editing to capture Yogananda's wisdom, his sense of fun, and his practical spiritual guidance.

How to Be Happy All the Time
The Wisdom of Yogananda Series, Volume 1
Paramhansa Yogananda

Yogananda powerfully explains virtually everything needed to lead a happier, more fulfilling life. Topics include: looking for happiness in the right places; choosing to be happy; tools and techniques for achieving happiness; sharing happiness with others; balancing success and happiness, and many more.

Karma and Reincarnation
The Wisdom of Yogananda Series, Volume 2
Paramhansa Yogananda

Yogananda reveals the truth behind karma, death, reincarnation, and the afterlife. With clarity and simplicity, he makes the mysterious understandable. Topics include: why we see a world of suffering and inequality; how to handle the challenges in our lives; what happens at death, and after death; and the origin and purpose of reincarnation.

Further Explorations

Spiritual Relationships
The Wisdom of Yogananda Series, Volume 3
Paramhansa Yogananda

Topics include: how to cure bad habits that spell the death of true friendship; how to choose the right partner and create a lasting marriage; sex in marriage and how to conceive a spiritual child; problems that arise in marriage and what to do about them; the divine plan uniting parents and children; the Universal Love behind all your relationships.

How to Be a Success
The Wisdom of Yogananda Series, Volume 4
Paramhansa Yogananda

This book includes the complete text of *The Attributes of Success*, the original booklet later published as *The Law of Success*. In addition, you will learn how to find your purpose in life, develop habits of success and eradicate habits of failure, develop your will power and magnetism, and thrive in the right job.

NEW in 2010
Another great title in the Yogananda Wisdom series!

How to Have Courage, Calmness, and Confidence

Further Explorations

Selections by Swami Kriyananda

The New Path
My Life with Paramhansa Yogananda
Swami Kriyananda

The New Path tells the story of a young American's spiritual quest, his discovery of the powerful classic, *Autobiography of a Yogi*, and his subsequent meeting with—and acceptance as a disciple by—the book's author, the great spiritual teacher and yoga master, Paramhansa Yogananda.

The New Path provides a marvelous sequel to Paramhansa Yogananda's own *Autobiography of a Yogi*, helping you to gain a more profound understanding of this great world teacher. Through hundreds of stories of life with Yogananda and through Swami Kriyananda's invaluable insights, you'll discover the inner path that leads to soul-freedom and lasting happiness.

Praise for *The New Path*

"Reading Autobiography of a Yogi *by Yogananda was a transformative experience for me and for millions of others. In* The New Path, *Kriyananda carries on this great tradition. Highly recommended."*—Dean Ornish, M.D., Founder and President, Preventative Medicine Research Institute, Clinical Professor of Medicine, University of California, San Francisco, author of *The Spectrum*

"Not only did Kriyananda walk in the footsteps of an enlightened master, The New Path *makes it obvious that he himself became an embodiment of Yogananda's teachings."*—Michael Bernard Beckwith, featured contributor to *The Secret,* and author of *Spiritual Liberation—Fulfilling Your Soul's Potential*

Further Explorations

Religion in the New Age
Swami Kriyananda

Our planet has entered an "Age of Energy"that will affect us for centuries to come. We can see evidence of this all around us: in ultra-fast computers, the quickening of communication and transportation, and the shrinking of time and space. This fascinating book of essays explores how this new age will change our lives, especially our spiritual seeking. Covers a wide range of upcoming societal shifts—in leadership, relationships, and self-development—including the movement away from organized religion to inner experience.

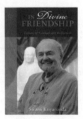

In Divine Friendship
Swami Kriyananda

This extraordinary book of nearly 250 letters, written over a thirty-year period by Swami Kriyananda, responds to practically any concern a spiritual seeker might have, such as: strengthening one's faith, accelerating one's spiritual progress, meditating more deeply, responding to illness, earning a living, attracting a mate, raising children, overcoming negative self-judgments, and responding to world upheavals.

Connecting all of these letters is the love, compassion, and wisdom of Swami Kriyananda, one of the leading spiritual figures of our times. The letters describe in detail his efforts to fulfill his Guru's commission to establish spiritual communities, and offer invaluable advice to leaders everywhere on how to avoid the temptations of materialism, selfishness, and pride. A spiritual treasure that speaks to spiritual seekers at all levels.

Meditation for Starters
Swami Kriyananda

Have you wanted to learn to meditate, but just never got around to it? Or tried "sitting in the silence" only to find yourself too restless to stay more than a few moments? If so, *Meditation for Starters* is just what you've been looking for, and with a companion CD, it provides everything you need to begin a meditation practice. It is filled with easy-to-follow instructions, beautiful guided visualizations, and answers to important questions on meditation, such as: what meditation is (and isn't); how to relax your body and prepare yourself for going within; and techniques for interiorizing and focusing the mind.

Awaken to Superconsciousness
How to Use Meditation for Inner Peace, Intuitive Guidance, and Greater Awareness
Swami Kriyananda

This popular guide includes everything you need to know about the philosophy and practice of meditation, and how to apply the meditative mind to resolving common daily conflicts in uncommon, superconscious ways. Superconsciousness is the source of intuition, spiritual healing, solutions to problems, and deep and lasting joy.

Praise for *Awaken to Superconsciousness*

"A brilliant, thoroughly enjoyable guide to the art and science of meditation. [Kriyananda] entertains, informs, and inspires—his enthusiasm for the subject is contagious. This book is a joy to read from beginning to end."—Yoga International

Also available in this series:
Music to Awaken Superconsciousness (CD)
Meditations to Awaken Superconsciousness, spoken word (CD)

Further Explorations

Affirmations for Self-Healing
Swami Kriyananda

This inspirational book contains fifty-two affirmations and prayers, each pair devoted to improving a quality in yourself. Strengthen your will power; cultivate forgiveness, patience, health, enthusiasm, and more. A powerful tool for self-transformation.

Praise for *Affirmations for Self-Healing*

"[Affirmations] *has become a meditation friend to me. The inspiring messages and prayers, plus the physical beauty of the book, help me start my day uplifted and focused.*"—Sue Patton Thoele, author of *Growing Hope*

ALSO AVAILABLE IN:
Audiobook (MP3 format)

Music and Audiobook Selections

Metaphysical Meditations
Swami Kriyananda

Kriyananda's soothing voice guides you in thirteen different meditations based on the soul-inspiring, mystical poetry of Paramhansa Yogananda. Each meditation is accompanied by beautiful classical music to help you quiet your thoughts and prepare for deep states of meditation. Includes a full recitation of Yogananda's poem "Samadhi," which appears in *Autobiography of a Yogi*. A great aid to the serious meditator, as well as to those just beginning their practice.

Further Explorations

Meditations to Awaken Superconsciousness
Guided Meditations on the Light
Swami Kriyananda

Featuring two beautiful guided meditations as well as an introductory section to help prepare the listener for meditation, this extraordinary recording of visualizations can be used either by itself, or as a companion to the book, *Awaken to Superconsciousness*. The soothing, transformative words, spoken over inspiring sitar background music, creates one of the most unique guided meditation products available.

Bliss Chants
Ananda Kirtan

Chanting focuses and lifts the mind to higher states of consciousness. *Bliss Chants* features chants written by Yogananda and his direct disciple, Swami Kriyananda. They're performed by Ananda Kirtan, a group of singers and musicians from Ananda, one of the world's most respected yoga communities. Chanting is accompanied by guitar, harmonium, kirtals, and tabla.

Other titles in the Chant Series:

Divine Mother Chants　　*Power Chants*
Love Chants　　*Peace Chants*
*Wisdom Chants**　　*Wellness Chants**

*Look for in 2010

Further Explorations

AUM: Mantra of Eternity
Swami Kriyananda

This recording features nearly seventy minutes of continuous vocal chanting of AUM, the Sanskrit word meaning peace and oneness of spirit. AUM, the cosmic creative vibration, is extensively discussed by Yogananda in *Autobiography of a Yogi*. Chanted here by his disciple, Kriyananda, this recording is a stirring way to tune into this cosmic power.

Other titles in the Mantra Series:

Gayatri Mantra*
Mahamrityanjaya Mantra*
Maha Mantra*

*Look for in 2010

We offer many of our book titles in unabridged MP3 format audiobooks. To purchase these titles and to see more music and audiobook offerings, visit our website www.crystalclarity.com. Or look for us in many of the popular online download sites.

Further Explorations

Crystal Clarity Publishers

When you're seeking a book on practical spiritual living, you want to know it's based on an authentic tradition of timeless teachings, and that it resonates with integrity. This is the goal of Crystal Clarity Publishers: to offer you books of practical wisdom filled with truc spiritual principles that have not only been tested through the ages, but also through personal experience.

We publish only books that combine creative thinking, universal principles, and a timeless message. Crystal Clarity books will open doors to help you discover more fulfillment and joy by living and acting from the center of peace within you.

Crystal Clarity Publishers—recognized worldwide for its bestselling, original, unaltered edition of Paramhansa Yogananda's classic *Autobiography of a Yogi*—offers many additional resources to assist you in your spiritual journey, including over ninety books, a wide variety of inspirational and relaxation music composed by Swami Kriyananda, Yogananda's direct disciple, and yoga and meditation DVDs.

For our online catalog, complete with secure ordering, please visit us on the web at:

www.crystalclarity.com

Further Explorations

Crystal Clarity music and audiobooks are available on the popular online download sites. Look for us on your favorite online music website.

To request a catalog, place an order for the products you read about in the Further Explorations section of this book, or to find out more information about us and our products, please contact us:

Contact Information

Crystal Clarity Publishers

14618 Tyler Foote Rd. • Nevada City, CA 95959

t: 800.424.1055 or 530.478.7600

w: www.crystalclarity.com

e: clarity@crystalclarity.com

Further Explorations

Ananda Sangha

Ananda Sangha is a fellowship of kindred souls following the teachings of Paramhansa Yogananda. The Sangha embraces the search for higher consciousness through the practice of meditation, and through the ideal of service to others in their quest for Self-realization. Approximately ten thousand spiritual seekers are affiliated with Ananda Sangha throughout the world.

Founded in 1968 by Swami Kriyananda, a direct disciple of Paramhansa Yogananda, Ananda includes seven communities in the United States, Europe, and in India. Worldwide, about one thousand devotees live in these spiritual communities, which are based on Yogananda's ideals of "plain living and high thinking."

"Thousands of youths must go north, south, east and west to cover the earth with little colonies, demonstrating that simplicity of living plus high thinking lead to the greatest happiness!" After pronouncing these words at a garden party in Beverly Hills, California in 1949, Paramhansa Yogananda raised his arms, and chanting the sacred cosmic vibration AUM, he "registered in the ether" his blessings on what has become the spiritual communities movement. From that moment on, Swami Kriyananda dedicated himself to bringing this vision from inspiration to reality by establishing communities where home, job, school, worship, family, friends, and recreation could evolve together as part of the interwoven fabric of harmonious, balanced living. Yogananda predicted that these communities would "spread like wildfire," becoming the model lifestyle for the coming millennium.

Swami Kriyananda lived with his guru during the last four years of the Master's life, and continued to serve his organization for another ten years, bringing the teachings of Kriya Yoga and Self-realization to audiences in the United States, Europe, Australia, and, from 1958–1962, India. In 1968, together with a small group of close friends and students, he founded the first "world-brotherhood community" in the foothills of the Sierra Nevada Mountains in northeastern California. Initially a meditation retreat center located on sixty-seven acres of forested land, Ananda World Brotherhood Village today encompasses one thousand acres where about 250 people live a dynamic, fulfilling life based on the principles and practices of spiritual, mental, and physical development, cooperation, respect, and divine friendship.

At this writing, after forty years of existence, Ananda is one of the most successful networks of intentional communities in the world. Urban communities have been developed in Palo Alto and Sacramento, California; Portland, Oregon; and Seattle, Washington. In Europe, near Assisi, Italy, a spiritual retreat and community was established in 1983, where today nearly one hundred residents from eight countries live. In Pune and Gurgaon, India there are two communities and a spiritual retreat center.

Further Explorations

Contact Information

Ananda Sangha

14618 Tyler Foote Rd. • Nevada City, CA 95959

t: 530.478.7560

w: www.ananda.org

e: sanghainfo@ananda.org

Further Explorations

The Expanding Light

Ananda's non-profit guest retreat, The Expanding Light, is visited by over two thousand people each year. We offer a varied, year-round schedule of classes and workshops on yoga, meditation, spiritual practices, yoga and meditation teacher training, and personal renewal retreats. The Expanding Light welcomes seekers from all backgrounds. Here you will find a loving, accepting environment, ideal for personal growth and spiritual renewal.

We strive to create an ideal relaxing and supportive environment for people to explore their own spiritual growth. We share the nonsectarian meditation practices and yoga philosophy of Paramhansa Yogananda and his direct disciple, Ananda's founder, Swami Kriyananda. Yogananda called his path "Self-realization," and our goal is to help our guests tune into their own higher Selves.

Contact Information

Expanding Light

14618 Tyler Foote Rd. • Nevada City, CA 95959

t: 800.346.5350

w: www.expandinglight.org

e: info@expandinglight.org

13364557

6714